这 在什么

dier - tra saan

CHENG & TSUI

"Bringing Asia to the World"™

趣学中文

Go Far
WITH CHINESE

Textbook 1B

Senior Curriculum Adviser
Ying Jin 金璎

Lead Instructional Contributors

Chunmei Guan 关春梅

Cilei Han 韩慈磊

Zoey Liu 刘喆医

Diane Neubauer 杜雁子

Erica Pollard 狄瑞和

CHENG & TSUI

"Bringing Asia to the World"™

First Edition 2021

24 23 22 21 20   1 2 3 4 5

ISBN 978-1-62291-064-9

Library of Congress Cataloging in
Publication data applied for.

Printed in Canada

The *Go Far with Chinese* series
encompasses textbooks, workbooks,
teacher's resources, audio, video, an
online edition on the ChengTsui Web App,
and more. Visit cheng-tsui.com for more
information on the other components of
Go Far with Chinese.

Publisher
JILL CHENG

Curriculum Development Manager
MEGAN BURNETT

Curriculum Development Staff
LEI WANG, TAMSIN TRUE-ALCALA,
EMILY PETIT, JINGGE LI, YINGCHUN
GUAN, AARON BALIVET

Managing Editor
KAESMENE HARRISON BANKS

Production Coordinator
TODD BROWN

Market and Photo Researchers
ELIZABETH HANLON, MARIAN STACEY

Cover Designers
CHRISTIAN SABOGAL with MARINA LI

Interior Designers
KATE PAPADAKI with MARINA LI

Comic Illustrator
MARGARET LOR

Photographs
© Cheng & Tsui
© Shutterstock

Photo credits are listed on p. 209

Cheng & Tsui Company, Inc.
25 West Street, Boston, MA 02111-1213 USA
P: 617.988.2400 / 800.554.1963
F: 617.426.3669
cheng-tsui.com

Series Contributors

Senior Curriculum Adviser

Ying Jin (金瓔) is a Chinese teacher in the Fremont Union High School District in California. She has more than 20 years of experience in Chinese instruction and is active in the teaching community through STARTALK, CLASS, California Language Teachers' Association, and more. In 2018, ACTFL named her the National Language Teacher of the Year, the first Chinese language teacher to receive this honor. She is passionate about promoting greater understanding of Chinese language and culture.

Lead Instructional Contributors

Chunmei Guan (关春梅) is a Chinese instructor at Logansport Community School Corporation in Indiana. She was named Chinese Teacher of the Year and earned the Outstanding Contribution award by the Indiana Chinese Language Teachers Association in 2016. She serves as the 2nd Vice-President of the Indiana Foreign Language Teachers Association and as an associate member of the National Council of State Supervisors for Languages. She also is a member of CLASS, CLTA-US, ACTFL, and ASSCE. She is dedicated to promoting cross-cultural and global awareness as an educator in the field of world language instruction.

Cilei Han (韩慈磊) is a teacher of Chinese language at Lake Oswego and Lakeridge High Schools in Oregon as well as a Challenge Program instructor at Portland State University. She serves as a board member of the Chinese Language Teachers Association, USA (CLTA-US), as chair of the CLTA K-12 Working Group, and as president of her regional Chinese Language Teachers Association-Oregon. She is dedicated to assisting in the development of stronger K-12 Chinese language programs nationwide.

Zoey Liu (刘喆医) teaches Chinese in the Fremont Union High School District in California. In 2017, she received the Yao Memorial Award for Outstanding New Teacher from CLASS. She is committed to helping students grow as global citizens by deepening their knowledge of Chinese language and culture.

Diane Neubauer (杜雁子), currently a PhD student in Foreign Language and ESL Education at the University of Iowa, has more than a decade of experience teaching Chinese at both elementary and secondary schools. She frequently conducts professional development workshops for language teachers and works to support and develop the community of Chinese teachers through her role as vice-chair of the ACTFL Comprehension-based Communicative Language Teaching Special Interest Group. She also regularly blogs about ideas and strategies for teaching Chinese.

Erica Pollard (狄瑞和) is the foreign language department director and an AP®[1] Chinese instructor at Hingham Public Schools in Massachusetts. She has extensive experience in curriculum design and has developed curricula for Chinese language courses from beginner to AP® levels. She also shares her teaching insights and knowledge through her work on the College Board's AP® Chinese Language and Culture Development Committee.

[1]AP® is a trademark registered by the College Board, which is not affiliated with, and does not endorse, this product.

Publisher's Note

Over the last four decades, Cheng & Tsui has grown from a scrappy distribution operation into a leading publisher of Chinese, Japanese, Korean, and Arabic language and culture materials, introducing Asia not only to America, but also to the rest of the world. We want to thank all of you, the many dedicated authors, staff, educators, and learners, who have made this milestone anniversary possible.

While we look back on past achievements — like the 1997 publication of the first edition of the global bestseller *Integrated Chinese*, followed by *Adventures in Japanese* in 1998 — we also look forward to a bright future. Over the years, trusting in our commitment to innovative, effective, and high quality language pedagogy, many educators have asked us for a new beginning Chinese textbook series for secondary school students. On our 40th anniversary, we are excited to answer this call with *Go Far with Chinese!*

You told us that you want a new textbook series that

- is innovative and effective;

- is age-appropriate, thematically-organized, and proficiency-based;

- offers careful vocabulary and grammar control;

- is designed with appropriate pacing and thoughtful articulation;

- provides robust support for teachers and students with authentic materials;

- is informed by the most current research on best practices in second language acquisition;

- is based on real classroom experiences of teachers and students;

- will have both print and online editions for hybrid and remote learning; and

- promises to lead new generations on a lifelong path to Chinese language learning!

In planning for such an ambitious project, we sought the advice and participation of outstanding teachers, researchers, and learners throughout America. Collaborating closely with our many advisers, Cheng & Tsui's highly dedicated and thoughtful curriculum development staff have made your requests a reality in *Go Far with Chinese!*

We know that it is difficult for any single textbook to meet the needs of every different kind of student audience and classroom setting. But as you use this material, we hope you will find that *Go Far with Chinese* provides enough structure and flexibility to make teaching easier and students' learning more fun and effective.

We truly believe that your success is our success, so we ask that you continue to let us know what you need and what you have on your wishlist. Only with your input can we continue to develop materials that will help you achieve your goals. Please contact your Cheng & Tsui account representative or editor@cheng-tsui.com with your suggestions.

All of us at Cheng & Tsui are grateful for your support!

Acknowledgments

Go Far with Chinese was developed thanks to the advice and contributions of countless educators from all across the United States. We would like to express our gratitude and appreciation to all those who contributed, including those listed below.

何仲健
Carol Bi
Boulder Creek High School
Anthem, Arizona

常小林
Xiaolin Chang, M.A.
Consultant to College Board
AP®2 Chinese, former Chair of the
Language Department
Lowell High School
San Francisco, California

趙哲瑩
Che-Ying Joy Chao
Woodbridge High School
Irvine, California

姜文静
Wenching Chiang
Sunset Ridge Middle School
East Hartford, Connecticut

董昕
Xin Dong, M.A.
Lincoln-Sudbury Regional
High School
Sudbury, Massachusetts

何小蔓
Mairead Harris, M.Ed.
Associate Director of the
Chinese School,
Middlebury Language Schools
Stowe Middle & High School
Stowe, Vermont

簡淑玲
Shwuling Jane
Jonas Clarke Middle School
Lexington, Massachusetts

景晓姝
Xiaoshu Jing, M.A.
Marlborough High School
Marlborough, Massachusetts

林玫
Mary Lane, M.A.
Tenafly Public Schools (retired)
Tenafly, New Jersey

李宜
Yi Lee
Henry J. Kaiser High School
Honolulu, Hawaii

李娜
Na Li, M.A.
Chinese Teacher and
World Language Curriculum
Coordinator
Columbus Academy
Gahanna, Ohio

林静容
Janet Lin
St. Mark's School of Texas Dallas,
Texas

刘兵
Bing Liu, M.A.
Metropolitan Learning Center
Bloomfield, Connecticut

刘伟
Wei Liu, PhD
The Hotchkiss School
Lakeville, Connecticut

卢文雅
Wenya Lu, M.A.
Teacher and Curriculum
Developer
Northside College
Preparatory High School
Chicago, Illinois

陳惠棻
Petra Lynch
Greenhill High School
Addison, Texas

秦莉杰
Lijie Qin, M.A.
Oak Hill Middle School
Newton, Massachusetts

芮尚勤
Dr. Reed Riggs
Brigham Young University–
Hawaii

史迪菲
Difei Shi
Tenakill Middle School
Closter, New Jersey

孙毅
Preston Sundin, M.A.
Emma Willard School
Troy, New York

吴萍
Ping Wu, M.Ed.
Columbus School for Girls
Columbus, Ohio

赖华睿
Reid Wyatt, M.A.T.
Brooks School
North Andover, Massachusetts

薛莉
Li Xue, M.A.
Wainwright Intermediate School
Fircrest, Washington

张世红
Shihong Zhang, M.A. & M.Ed.
Glen Ridge High School
Glen Ridge, New Jersey

*All Chinese names are listed in accordance with the way they were provided.

2AP® is a trademark registered by the College Board, which is not affiliated with, and does not endorse, this product.

Contents

Unit 2: School Life

Chapter 4: Too Many Classes!

Chapter 5: How's It Going?

Chapter 6: Taking Care of Yourself

Preface

The origins of *Go Far with Chinese* are firmly rooted in the experience of Chinese teachers and students at the secondary school level. The series covers three to four years of beginning Chinese language instruction in a traditional U.S. secondary school setting. Levels 1A and 1B teach the same content as Level 1, but are designed to be used for two years at the middle school level or in high school programs with fewer instructional hours. Unit 1 in Level 1B is unique in that the Chapters in Unit 1 are shorter and introduce fewer new vocabulary words and less grammar than is typical of the series. This allows for greater focus on reviewing the vocabulary and grammar taught in Level 1A. Students who complete the three-level series will be ready to study the widely used *Integrated Chinese* series Volumes 3 and 4 either for AP®[3] preparation or at the college level. Upon completing *Go Far with Chinese* students will be able to confidently embark on their own language learning journeys.

Foundational Ideas

The curriculum of *Go Far with Chinese* was developed in accordance with the best practices defined by current research in second language acquisition. In particular, the curriculum is fully aligned to the World-Readiness Standards and Guiding Principles for Language Learning recommended by the American Council on the Teaching of Foreign Languages (ACTFL). Below are some of the foundational ideas that shaped the program.

Proficiency-Based Instruction

Go Far with Chinese places strong emphasis on real-world communication—that is, on what students can actually *do* with the language they have learned. Using a backward design process, the curriculum development team first identified language and cultural content learning goals, and then used those goals to write the comic stories at the end of each Chapter. The team then outlined Unit-level Integrated Performance Assessments and worked with expert Chinese language educators from across the United States to plan the task-based learning experiences and instructional materials that would help students reach those goals.

Vocabulary Control

Careful attention was paid to vocabulary control. High-frequency "function" words, such as 想, 喜欢, and 去, are introduced early to give students the ability to have authentic conversations about their likes, wants, and plans. In addition, the program also prioritizes vocabulary relevant to students' lives, such as words related to pets, families, sports, and music.

Grammar in Context

Current research indicates that the most effective method for teaching grammar is to present it in context, focusing on the communicative meaning of a form rather than on explaining the form itself. In the Textbook, students are encouraged to get the gist of the meaning of new language before focusing on the details of form.

[3]AP® is a trademark registered by the College Board, which is not affiliated with, and does not endorse, this product.

Emphasis on Meaning-Based Tasks & Activities

Go Far with Chinese emphasizes authentic communicative tasks that ask students to express ideas and opinions, rather than formulaic drills or rehearsed exercises. Practice sections in the Textbook move from brief, semi-guided exercises to independent tasks designed to elicit meaning-based communication.

Literacy & Character Learning

While literacy instruction should be an integral part of any beginning Chinese program, there is also a clear need to set realistic goals given the challenges of learning a new writing system. *Go Far with Chinese* is designed to support literacy instruction while giving teachers flexibility with regard to writing assignments. For example, students are expected to learn to read and write only the words in the vocabulary lists, while word banks throughout the Textbook provide supplemental vocabulary. Pinyin is provided for new words and then phased out over the course of each Section to help students develop strong reading skills. To accelerate students' word recognition, *Go Far with Chinese* explicitly teaches recurring components, with the stroke order for characters given in the Character Workbook. Students can answer open-ended questions in the Textbook and Workbook either by typing or hand writing their responses, as teachers direct.

Use of Target Language

To help achieve ACTFL's goal for teachers to conduct 90% of classroom learning in the target language, *Go Far with Chinese* teaches students useful classroom phrases early on. Additional comprehensible input strategies provided in the Teacher's Resources also help maximize students' exposure to Chinese during class time.

Personalization

In order to increase student interest and create opportunities for real-world communication, activities and exercises were designed to relate to students' lives and to encourage them to express their own ideas and opinions. Additionally, the Teacher's Resources suggest ways to tap into students' specific interests and adapt classroom content accordingly.

Stories as a Teaching Tool

The final Section of each Chapter combines the new language students have studied in an engaging comic story. Age- and level-appropriate plots foster student interest and engagement. The stories in *Go Far with Chinese* are presented in dialogue format to keep the focus on informal spoken language and to model natural exchanges.

Authentic Materials

The ACTFL Guiding Principles for Language Learning encourage the use of authentic materials even in the beginning stage of language learning. Tasks based on realia, photos, and videos of China help students build cultural literacy and develop the ability to analyze authentic materials.

References

Adair-Hauck, Bonnie, Eileen W. Glisan, and Francis J. Troyan. *Implementing Integrated Performance Assessment.* Alexandria, VA: American Council on the Teaching of Foreign Languages, 2013.

Clementi, Donna, and Laura Terrill. *The Keys to Planning for Learning, Second Edition.* Alexandria, VA: American Council on the Teaching of Foreign Languages, 2017.

"Guiding Principles for Language Learning." The American Council on the Teaching of Foreign Languages. Accessed August 6, 2019. https://www.actfl.org/guiding-principles

Hadley, Alice Omaggio. *Teaching Language in Context, Third Edition.* Boston: Heinle & Heinle, 2001.

Mart, Cagri. "Teaching Grammar in Context: Why and How?" *Theory and Practice in Language Studies* Vol. 3, No. 1 (2013): 124-129.

Rezende Lucarevschi, Claudio. "The Role of Storytelling on Language Learning: A Literature Review." *Working Papers of the Linguistic Circle of the University of Victoria* Vol. 26, No. 1 (2016): 23-44

VanPatten, Bill. *While We're On the Topic.* Alexandria, VA: American Council on the Teaching of Foreign Languages, 2017.

Wong, Wynn and Bill VanPatten. "The Evidence is IN: Drills are OUT." *Foreign Language Annals* Vol. 36, No. 3 (2003): 403-423.

Waltz, Terry. *TPRS with Chinese Characteristics.* Squid for Brains Educational Publishing, 2015.

Textbook Organization

Each Level in *Go Far with Chinese* includes a Textbook, Workbook, Character Workbook, audio, video, and Teacher's Resources.

Level 1B is divided into three thematic Units consisting of three Chapters each. In every Unit, a broad, thought-provoking Essential Question challenges students to reflect on how they view language, their own culture and other cultures, and the world at large. Unit Projects, in the form of Integrated Performance Assessments (IPAs), test students' ability to understand and use the language they have learned in a real-world scenario.

Each Chapter of *Go Far with Chinese* follows a tiered approach to instruction: students move from processing teacher-provided comprehensible input to brief, semi-guided exercises, and finally to independent tasks. To keep the pace manageable, the target vocabulary and grammar are divided and introduced over the first few Sections of each Chapter. The final Section, Put the Pieces Together, combines the Chapter's new vocabulary and grammar into a comic story and provides additional projects to round out the Chapter.

Can-Do Goals

Each Chapter begins with Can-Do Goals to set clear expectations for what students will learn to do in the three modes of communication. The Can-Do Goals are restated at the end of each Chapter so students can check their own progress and take ownership of their learning.

Culture Connection

This feature opens a window into contemporary Chinese culture, highlighting cultural products and practices that influence the daily lives of students' Chinese peers. Relatable and interesting content, full-color authentic photographs, topical words and expressions, and reflection questions all help students explore the Unit's Essential Question and build intercultural competence.

Language Model [Target Language Input]

The images on the Language Model pages can be used in conjunction with PowerPoint presentations in the Teacher's Resources to introduce the target structures and vocabulary for the Section through interactive class discussion. This ensures that students' exposure to the new language comes in a meaningful context through comprehensible input.

New Words in Conversation/Context [Interpretive]

In New Words in Conversation/Context, the Section's vocabulary and grammar are presented in a single, cohesive dialogue or passage. Students first listen to the audio and try to grasp the gist of the meaning based on the language input they received during the Language Model discussion. Then, with the aid of the pinyin text and vocabulary list, they read the dialogue or passage, deepening their comprehension and connecting the new language to its written form.

Puzzle It Out [Progress Check]

Students complete these exercises to check their comprehension of the language points presented in Language Model and New Words in Conversation/Context.

Language Reference

Clear explanations, presented alongside helpful visuals, serve as a reference for students to consult to clarify and consolidate their understanding of new grammar and word usage. The language points are presented contextually as ways to convey meaning, rather than as rules to be memorized.

Using the Language [Interpersonal/Presentational]

Interactive tasks elicit spontaneous, unscripted conversation between students by creating situations with a genuine communicative need. Some Using the Language activities are designed to be followed by a class discussion, giving students an opportunity to speak presentationally on the topic at hand. Others consist of games or puzzles that provide a clear communicative goal to encourage interaction.

Put the Pieces Together!

In the final Section, students first read a comic that combines the new language of the Chapter in a single, engaging story. Then, students complete additional exercises covering all three modes of communication to consolidate their grasp of Chapter content and to prepare for the Unit level IPA. Each Put the Pieces Together Section features an interpretive exercise built on authentic materials as well as a final project that asks students to work collaboratively on a presentational performance or piece of writing. In addition, the following three floating features appear at least once in each Chapter.

Language Challenge

The Language Challenge gives motivated and more advanced students an additional opportunity to apply their new language skills and personalize their learning. Teachers can use the Language Challenge as extra credit or as a way to differentiate instruction, providing an activity for advanced or heritage students who are moving more quickly than their peers.

5Cs

This feature expands on topics that emerge in the Chapter, integrating the 5Cs into the flow of language instruction and helping teachers effectively implement the ACTFL World-Readiness Standards for Language Learning.

What a Character!

Students are introduced to common radicals and character components that appear in some words in a Chapter, resulting in an integrated, context-driven foray into character analysis.

Scope & Sequence

Unit 1: Exploring Beijing

Essential Question: If you had a chance to take a trip, how would you decide what to see, eat, and do?

Chapter	Can-Do Goals	Language Points
Chapter 1: A Taste of Beijing **Culture Connection:** **Local Eats** 当地美食	• Name some foods that are popular in China • Talk about what you eat for breakfast • Describe other people's food preferences • Discuss which foods and how much food to order • Provide additional details and options	• Review: Word order with time expressions • Review: Expressing wants and intentions with 要 • 还 vs. 也
Chapter 2: Places to Visit **Culture Connection:** **Must-See Beijing Sites** 北京必去景点	• Name some famous Beijing tourist attractions and understand their importance, both historically and for the people of China today • Understand descriptions of tourist attractions • Tell others your impressions of different tourist attractions • Express strong opinions	• Review: Using 有 to show existence • Review: Linking descriptions to nouns with 的 • Expressing a strong feeling with 太...了
Chapter 3: Let's Go! **Events and Festivals** 盛会和节庆	• Recognize some famous sites and events in China • Discuss activities that are allowed (or not allowed) in certain locations • Describe events that are fun to attend • Understand and make comparisons	• Review: 可以 vs. 会 • Using 比 and 更 to make comparisons

Unit 2: School Life

Essential Question: How is student life similar throughout the world?

Chapter	Can-Do Goals	Language Points
Chapter 4: Too Many Classes! **Culture Connection: Educational Choices** 学业选择	• Understand and compare the Chinese school system to your own • Talk about your favorite classes • Compare and contrast different things • Tell someone what you are about to do • Express both strong and weak opinions • Describe someone's feelings	• Using 哪 to ask which • Expressing that something is about to happen with 要...了 • Using 挺...的 to indicate degree
Chapter 5: How's It Going? **Culture Connection: Student Life** 学生生活	• Discuss the specific time of an activity or event • Understand when others talk about running later than expected • Talk about what you need to do every day or every week • Talk about doing things with other people • Express how you are the same as or different from someone else • Understand aspects of student life in China and compare them to your own experience	• The basics of telling time • Expressing that something happened later than expected with 才 • Expressing "every" with 每...都 • Talking about what you have to do with 得 • Talking about doing things with someone with 跟...(一起) • Saying things are the same or alike with 跟/和...一样
Chapter 6: Taking Care of Yourself **Culture Connection: Student Health** 学生健康	• Understand what Chinese students might do to stay healthy • Talk about what you can do and what the situation allows you to do • Discuss adjusting plans to do something a bit earlier or later • Understand when others say they are hungry, thirsty, hot, or cold • Talk about common health problems • Express what you do (and do not do) when you are sick	• Stating what you are able to do with 能 • Expressing "a bit" with (一)点儿 • Using 有(一)点儿 to express "a bit, kind of" • Using 的 to link something to a phrase that describes it • Describing a specific time or situation with 的时候

Unit 3: A Balanced Schedule

Essential Question: How do you decide what to spend time on outside of class?

Chapter	Can-Do Goals	Language Points
Chapter 7: Looking for Support **Culture Connection:** **Academic Support** 学习辅助	• Understand ways Chinese students might look for academic support • Discuss doing something again • Understand when someone describes a sequence of events • Talk about completing a task • Advise someone to do more or less of something • Express things that will happen or that could happen	• Saying that something is still the case using 还 • Using 又 and 再 • Describing completing or finishing something with 完 • Indicating more and less using 多 and 少 • Expressing a change in situation with 了 • Talking about possible events with 会
Chapter 8: Making Progress **Culture Connection:** **The Arts and Chinese Learning** 艺术和中文学习	• Explore fun activities to support learning Chinese outside the classroom • Describe your impression of different activities • Say that you or others were mistaken in their thinking • Discuss what you have done before • Understand when someone emphasizes what something is or who someone is • Describe how a situation changes over time	• Indicating an impression or judgement with 起来 • Using 过 to talk about a past experience • Emphasizing what something is or who someone is with 就 • Using 越来越 to express "more and more"
Chapter 9: School and Activities **Culture Connection:** **Student Clubs** 学生俱乐部	• Name some of the types of student clubs available in Chinese schools • Discuss joining student clubs • Understand when others express how well they do something • Make contrasting statements • Talk about something you are hoping for	• Describing the way you do something with 得 • Verb and object as a detachable compound • Expressing contrasting statements using 虽然... 但是...

Audio

This icon indicates that audio content is available. Audio can be downloaded at cheng-tsui.com.

Cast of Characters

The Lopezes live in a very international neighborhood in Beijing. Here are some of their friends and neighbors. Their conversations throughout the book will help introduce you to the Chinese language.

Isabella Lopez, 16, from the United States

Martin Lopez, 14, from the United States

Emma Lopez, Isabella and Martin's mother

Daming Bai, Isabella and Martin's friend and Chinese tutor

Leo Fischer, 14, from Germany

Mr. Fischer, Leo's father

Miko Futamura, 16, from Japan

Sanjay Patel, 15, from the United States

Ellen Jones, 16, from the United Kingdom

Maya Young, 14, from the United States

Owen Kang, 16, from the United States

EXPLORING BEIJING

In Unit 1, you will discuss some Beijing tourist attractions and learn more ways to talk about food and activities. You will also learn to compare things and express strong opinions.

Beijing National Stadium – also called the Bird's Nest – in the evening

Essential Question

If you had a chance to take a trip, how would you decide what to see, eat, and do?

CHAPTER 1
A Taste of Beijing

As part of her summer homework, Isabella introduces herself and talks about her move to Beijing.

CHAPTER 2
Places to Visit

Daming, Martin, and Isabella talk about which tourist attractions in Beijing they find interesting.

CHAPTER 3
Let's Go!

On their way to the Great Wall, Isabella and Martin ask their friends about what they enjoy doing in Beijing.

UNIT 1 PROJECT

At the end of the unit, you will imagine that you are preparing to visit Beijing with a classmate and need to create an itinerary. You will:

- Read two blog posts that mention a variety of things one can do in Beijing

- Work in pairs to decide which activities you both want to do

- Present your itinerary to your classmates

A Taste of Beijing

Martin: Time flies! I can't believe there's less than a month before Daming goes back to the U.S. and we start school here in China.

Isabella: Wait, less than a month?! I still have summer homework to do. I guess I'd better get started on that soon!

Martin: Probably. I finished mine last week.

Isabella: It's been an interesting summer. I'll have plenty to write about!

Can-Do Goals

In this chapter, you will learn to:

- Name some foods that are popular in China
- Talk about what you eat for breakfast
- Describe other people's food preferences
- Discuss which foods and how much food to order
- Provide additional details and options

当地美食
dāngdì   měishí
Local Eats

Trying new foods is a major part of the travel experience. But don't expect the food you find in China to taste like the Chinese food you've eaten at home! In many cases, the food served in Chinese restaurants outside of China has been adjusted to suit local tastes. This means that a lot of the food you can find in China might be new to you!

Breakfast Options

This shop in Shanghai is selling some popular, grab-and-go Chinese breakfast foods: 包子 (bāozi), steamed buns with a bready outside and a sweet or savory filling; 煮玉米 (zhǔ yùmǐ), corn on the cob; and 茶叶蛋 (cháyèdàn), eggs hard-boiled in a mixture of tea, soy sauce, and spices.

Roast Duck

Peking duck, or 北京烤鸭 (Běijīng kǎoyā), is considered a signature Beijing dish. Diners top the sliced duck with sauce and scallions and then wrap it in a tortilla-like crepe to eat. This chef is carving a duck right at the table!

Social Food

Cooking at the table is a popular group dining activity. Hot pot, or 火锅 (huǒguō), is a fun and social dish to eat with other people. A pot of boiling broth is placed in the center of the table, and diners order vegetables, meat, tofu, noodles, or other ingredients to cook in it. Everyone adds their ingredients to the simmering broth, fishing them out once they are cooked.

By the Numbers

Travelers to China might notice pork reigns supreme in Chinese cuisine. About seven times more pork than beef is consumed per capita (that is, per person) in China. Here's how China's consumption of different types of meat compares with that of some other countries.

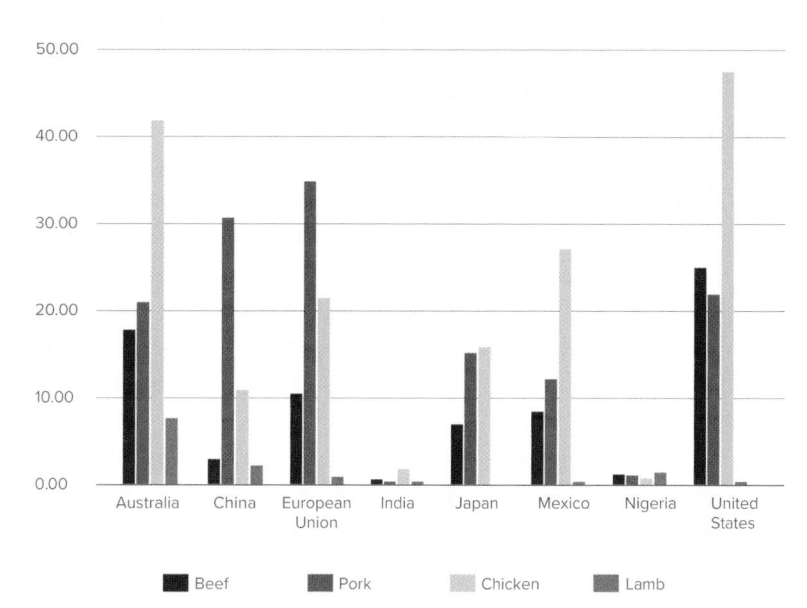

Types of Meat Consumed Per Capita in 2017 (kg)

Source: Organization for Economic Co-operation and Development, 2019

REFLECT ON THE ESSENTIAL QUESTION

If you had a chance to take a trip, how would you decide what to see, eat, and do?

1. Do you think food is an important part of a culture? Why or why not?

2. Are there any regional dishes that you think a visitor to your home state should be sure to try? Which one(s) and why?

3. If you were planning a trip, would trying local food be on your itinerary?

Talking about food choices

1a Language Model TARGET LANGUAGE INPUT

Your teacher will lead a discussion about the images below. Try to participate as much as you can. If there is anything you don't understand, let your teacher know.

Nǐ	zǎoshàng	xǐhuan	chī	shénme?
你	早上	喜欢	吃	什么?

What do you like to eat in the morning?
(What do you like to eat for breakfast?)

1

yùmǐpiàn

玉米片

cornflakes

2

shuǐguǒ

水果

fruit

3

bāozi

包子

baozi

1b New Words in Conversation `INTERPRETIVE`

Audio

Listen to the audio and try to understand as much as you can. Then read the dialogue, using the pinyin text and vocabulary list to figure out unfamiliar words.

 今天早上你们想吃什么？ Jīntiān zǎoshàng nǐmen xiǎng chī shénme?

 我要吃玉米片和水果。 Wǒ yào chī yùmǐpiàn hé shuǐguǒ.

 我今天不太想吃玉米片， Wǒ jīntiān bú tài xiǎng chī yùmǐpiàn,
我想吃包子…… wǒ xiǎng chī bāozi...

 包子很好吃！妈妈， Bāozi hěn hǎochī! Māma,
我也想吃包子。 wǒ yě xiǎng chī bāozi.

 春月，那你去买包子吧！ Chūnyuè, nà nǐ qù mǎi bāozi ba!

 你去吧，马丁！ Nǐ qù ba, Mǎdīng!

Comprehension Check

		T	F
1	At first, Martin says he wants to eat cornflakes.	○	○
2	In the end, Isabella and Martin both want to eat baozi.	○	○

Vocabulary

Audio

	Word	Pinyin	Meaning
1	玉米片	yùmǐpiàn	cornflakes
2	水果	shuǐguǒ	fruit
3	包子	bāozi	baozi

1c Puzzle It Out PROGRESS CHECK

Complete the exercises below to check your understanding of what you reviewed in Section 1. If you have questions, consult the Language Review section.

Exercise 1 Where in the following sentences can the time phrases be added?

1 (1) 你 (2) 有空吗？

   (a) 星期五晚上 can only be added where (1) is.

   (b) 星期五晚上 can be added either where (1) is or where (2) is.

2 我 (1) 要去给我朋友买生日礼物 (2)。

   (a) 明天下午 can only be added where (1) is.

   (b) 明天下午 can be added either where (1) is or where (2) is.

Exercise 2 Use the words in the list on the left to complete the translation of the sentences. You may use some words more than once.

要
不
不要
不想

1 她　　　　去买书，她　　　　去打篮球。
   She's not going to buy books; she's going to play basketball.

2 他今天早上　　　　吃玉米片，他　　　　吃包子。
   He doesn't want to have cornflakes for breakfast. He wants to have baozi.

3 我　　　　这个，我　　　　那个。
   I don't want this. I want that.

Language Review

1 Word order with time expressions

Time expressions in Chinese can come before the subject or after the subject, but unlike in English, time expressions cannot come at the end of the sentence.

   bāozi
1 我今天早上想吃包子。
   I want to have baozi (for breakfast) this morning.

2 我们星期五晚上去看电影吧！
   Let's go see a movie Friday night!

3 下个周末你不在家吗？
   Won't you be home next weekend?

2 Meanings and uses of 要

要 has several different meanings. In one usage, 要 can mean that someone is "going to (do something)." Reminder: 要 is left out when saying that someone is not going to do something.

1 她明天要去打篮球。

She is going to play basketball tomorrow.

2 她明天不去打篮球。

She is not going to play basketball tomorrow.

要 can also mean "to want (to do something)." This use is similar to 想, but using 要 shows that the speaker is more certain that he or she will do that activity. A speaker will usually use 要 if he or she has a plan in place or is ready to act. When saying that someone does not want to do something, 想 is used more often than 要.

3 我要买这种水果。
　　shuǐguǒ

I want to buy this type of fruit (and I'm going to!).

4 我不想买这种水果。
　　　shuǐguǒ

I don't want to buy this type of fruit.

A third meaning of 要 is "to want (something)." With this usage, the sentence can be negated with 不要.

5 我要这本书。

I want this book.

6 我不要那本书。

I don't want that book.

LANGUAGE CHALLENGE

You learned the word 饭馆 previously. Based on the words below, what do you think 饭 could mean?

zǎofàn
早饭
breakfast

Wǔfàn
午饭
lunch

wǎnfàn
晚饭
dinner

1d Using the Language INTERPERSONAL

Activity 1 Imagine that your school is launching a breakfast program and wants to know more about what students like to eat in the morning. In groups, interview each other in Chinese about your breakfast preferences, tally the results, and create a bar graph to report the outcomes. Ask your teacher or check a dictionary to find additional Chinese words for breakfast foods that you want to include in your survey.

Example:

A: 你早上喜欢吃什么？

B: 我早上喜欢吃玉米片！

Activity 2 Imagine that you are preparing a group order for breakfast at a Chinese restaurant.

Step 1: Choose the foods you want from the menu below, and decide how many of each food you want for yourself.

Step 2: Your teacher will assign you to a group and select a group leader and a notetaker. The group leader will ask the other students what foods they want and how many of each they want to order. The notetaker will keep track of each student's response and calculate the total number of each food requested by the group.

Step 3: When you have your final numbers, let your teacher know how many of each food you are going to order, using the phrase 我们要点 …

Useful phrases:

你想吃什么？

你要几个 ＿＿＿＿＿？

老师，我们要点 ＿＿＿＿＿。

bāozi
包子
¥2 /个

zhǔ yùmǐ
煮玉米
¥2 /个

jiānbǐng
煎饼
¥3.5 /个

cháyèdàn
茶叶蛋
¥1.5 /个

Asking "what else" with 还

2a Language Model [TARGET LANGUAGE INPUT]

Your teacher will lead a discussion about the images below. Try to participate as much as you can. If there is anything you don't understand, let your teacher know.

Zhège	fànguǎn	hái	yǒu	shénme
这个	饭馆	还	有	什么

hǎochī	de	cài?
好吃	的	菜?

What other tasty dishes does this restaurant serve (have)?

1

kǎoyā
烤鸭
roast duck

2

huǒguō
火锅
hot pot

Audio

2b New Words in Context INTERPRETIVE

Listen to Sanjay talk about his family's upcoming dinner plans and try to understand as much as you can. Then read the passage below, using the pinyin text and vocabulary list to figure out unfamiliar words.

这个星期五晚上我们要去小明饭馆吃饭。我喜欢吃烤鸭，我爸爸也喜欢吃烤鸭，所以我要点一份烤鸭。我爸爸还喜欢吃火锅。我和弟弟都不喜欢吃火锅，所以我不想点火锅。这个饭馆还有什么好吃的菜？

Zhège xīngqīwǔ wǎnshàng wǒmen yào qù Xiǎomíng Fànguǎn chī fàn. Wǒ xǐhuan chī kǎoyā, wǒ bàba yě xǐhuan chī kǎoyā, suǒyǐ wǒ yào diǎn yí fèn kǎoyā. Wǒ bàba hái xǐhuan chī huǒguō. Wǒ hé dìdi dōu bù xǐhuan chī huǒguō, suǒyǐ wǒ bù xiǎng diǎn huǒguō. Zhège fànguǎn hái yǒu shénme hǎochī de cài?

Comprehension Check

		T	F
1	Sanjay will order roast duck at Xiaoming Restaurant.	○	○
2	Sanjay wants to eat hot pot tonight.	○	○

Audio

Vocabulary

	Word	Pinyin	Meaning
4	饭	fàn	meal, cooked rice
5	烤鸭	kǎoyā	roast duck
6	还	hái	also, in addition, too, as well
7	火锅	huǒguō	hot pot

What a Character!

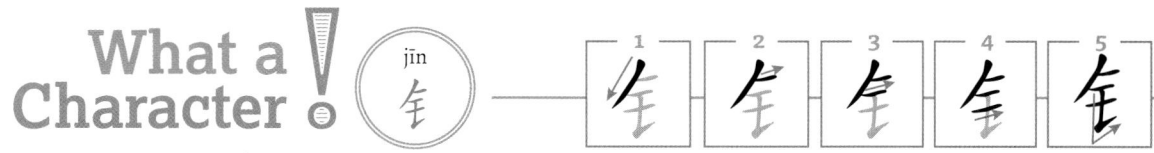

jīn 金

The character 金 (jīn), which means "gold," often appears as the component 钅 (jīn) on the left side of a character. Characters with this component usually have something to do with metal (not necessarily gold).

With the help of the images, can you guess what these three characters mean?

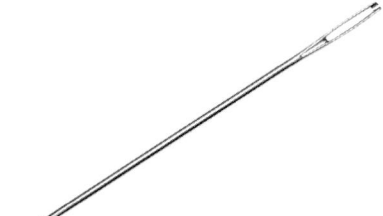

1 钟 (zhōng)　　　**2** 针 (zhēn)　　　**3** 钱 (qián)

2c Puzzle It Out   PROGRESS CHECK

Complete the exercise below to check your understanding of what you learned in Section 2. If you have questions, consult the Language Reference section.

Which word should be added to the following sentences? Choose 也 or 还.

也　　还

two dotted eel

1 他会做菜，我 ___ 会做菜。
He knows how to cook, and I also know how to cook.

⊙　　⊙

adding on

2 这个书店 ___ 有什么有意思的书？
What other interesting books does this bookstore have?

○　　

3 我不喜欢踢足球，我弟弟 ___ 不
喜欢踢足球。
I don't like to play soccer, and my younger brother also doesn't like to play soccer.

○　　◉

1 还 vs. 也 *in addition to*

还 (hái) and 也 can both mean "also," and they are often interchangeable. However, only 也 is used when discussing two different people or topics, as shown in bold below.

1 我很喜欢听音乐。我妹妹也很喜欢听音乐。

I really like listening to music. **My younger sister** also really likes listening to music.

In questions that use the word "else" or "other," use 还 (hái), not 也. When you are asked a question using 还 (hái), it is best to respond with 还 (hái).

2 A: 我想点面条。

I want to order noodles.

B: 好。你^{hái}还想点什么(菜)?

Okay, what else (what other dish) do you want to order?

A: 我^{hái}还想点^{kǎoyā}烤鸭!

I (also) want to order roast duck!

5Cs CONNECTIONS
COMMUNITIES
COMMUNICATION
CULTURES
COMPARISONS

You now know that characters with the 钅 (jīn) component often have something to do with metal. Take a look at this section of the Periodic Table of Elements and try to find an element that is a metal.

					2 He 氦
5 B 硼	6 C 碳	7 N 氮	8 O 氧	9 F 氟	10 Ne 氖
13 Al 铝	14 Si 硅	15 P 磷	16 S 硫	17 Cl 氯	18 Ar 氩

2d Using the Language INTERPERSONAL

Play a guessing game with a partner. Pick one of the 饭馆 below and pretend you're there — but keep your location a secret! To win, you must correctly guess which restaurant your partner is at before your partner guesses which restaurant you are at. If you guess wrong, you automatically lose!

● Start your turn by saying 那个饭馆有什么菜？

● After your partner answers the question, your partner gets a turn to ask you.

● When it is your turn again, you can ask 那儿还有什么菜？ Your partner must reply with something else served at that restaurant. Once you feel confident that you know where your partner is, guess!

 红烧肉，火锅，肉包子，饺子，面条

 饺子，肉包子，面条，烤鸭，水果

 烤鸭，肉包子，饺子，菜包子

 火锅，烤鸭，红烧肉，水果

 面条，火锅，烤鸭，肉包子，菜包子

 玉米，肉包子，菜包子，水果

Put the Pieces Together!

 Audio

A Reading and Listening INTERPRETIVE

Passage 1

ISABELLA IS SITTING AT HER DESK, WRITING.

我叫春月。

这是我弟弟。
他的中文名字是马丁。

他是大明。
他家和我们家
在一个小区。

我们是美国人。
可是，现在我们和妈妈在中国！

他现在是我和马丁的中文老师，
也是我们的好朋友。

他教我们中文，
也教我弹一种
中国乐器——
古筝。

大明很喜欢吉他。

马丁现在教大明弹吉他，
可是我觉得他不是一个好老师。

我们都很喜欢听中国音乐、打乒乓球，
还很喜欢吃中国菜！

在美国，我早上
经常吃玉米片。
现在在北京，
我早上很喜欢吃包子！

我还很喜欢吃烤鸭和火锅！

17

11 可是，经常去饭馆吃饭很贵，所以周末我们经常和妈妈去学做中国菜。

12 nǐ hǎo zhōng guó
你好中国

现在，我很喜欢学中文，很喜欢中国，还很喜欢做中国菜！

Comprehension Check

		T	F
1	Isabella and Martin live in the same neighborhood as Daming.	○	○
2	Isabella often had cornflakes for breakfast in America.	○	○
3	Isabella does not like roast duck.	○	○
4	Martin and Emma are learning to cook, but Isabella is not.	○	○

Passage 2 This instant food is found at a supermarket in Chinatown. What do you think it is?

Bonus: Research how to prepare this food and share what you learn with the class.

Passage 3 Listen to the conversation, then answer the following questions.

1 What does the boy like to eat for breakfast?

    (a) just baozi
    (b) cornflakes and fruit
    (c) baozi, cornflakes, and fruit

2 What does the girl like to eat for breakfast?

    (a) baozi
    (b) fruit
    (c) cornflakes

3 What do you think the girl's favorite dish is?

    (a) roast duck
    (b) noodles
    (c) hot pot

Passage 4 Listen to the conversation between the man and the woman. Based on their conversation, which three foods will they order?

A   B   C   D

B Speaking INTERPERSONAL

Learn more about a classmate's meal preferences! Ask your partner which restaurant he/she would like to eat breakfast at, which restaurant he/she would like to eat lunch at, and why. Be prepared to share the answers with your class. Which restaurants seem to be most popular?

A

A restaurant in Beijing

B

A food stand in Hangzhou

C

A food stand in Chengdu

D

A sign advertising the menu at a cafe

C Final Project PRESENTATIONAL

Cultural Appreciation Week

Imagine that your class has decided to make and sell Chinese food during your school's cultural appreciation week in order to raise money for a trip to Chinatown. However, you're not sure which dishes will sell well at the event.

Step 1: To get ideas, find a menu from a Chinese restaurant or use one of the menus in this book. In groups, look at the menu and discuss which Chinese dishes you want to sell. Create a list, and then use this list to survey other students in your class about their preferences.

Step 2: Once you know which dishes are most popular, create a poster showing the foods you will sell at your stand. Write the names of the dishes in both Chinese and English. Get creative: Make your stall seem more authentic by giving it a Chinese name, adding a promotional Chinese slogan to the poster, and putting up Chinese decorations. Make sure that your stall is eye-catching!

Students at Logansport High School making wontons and dumplings.

Can-Do Goals

Talk with your teacher if you have questions or if you are not certain you can do the following tasks:

- Name some foods that are popular in China
- Talk about what you eat for breakfast
- Describe other people's food preferences
- Discuss which foods and how much food to order
- Provide additional details and options

Cultural Knowledge

What are some foods that are popular in Beijing?

A vendor at the Wangfujing street food market in Beijing

Places to Visit

Isabella: Our cooking class this weekend got canceled. I guess we'll have more free time!

Martin: Great! That means we can...watch more TV?

Isabella: I'm tired of watching TV.

Martin: Yeah, me too.... Hey, it's almost time for us to meet up with Daming to play ping-pong!

Isabella: Oh, right — I guess we should get going! And maybe Daming will have ideas for things to do this weekend!

Can-Do Goals

In this chapter, you will learn to:

- Name some famous Beijing tourist attractions and understand their importance, both historically and for the people of China today

- Understand descriptions of tourist attractions

- Tell others your opinions of different tourist attractions

- Express strong opinions

Běijīng bì qù jǐngdiǎn
北京必去景点
Must-See Beijing Sites

Beijing is not only China's capital and largest city, it is home to some of China's most famous historic sites. If you visit Beijing, you won't want to miss these three classic attractions!

The Great Wall

Thousands of years ago, walls were built in northern China to defend against attack. In the 3rd century BCE these walls were joined together, creating the Great Wall, or 长城 (Chángchéng). After continuous rebuilding and additions over the centuries, the wall came to extend some 5,500 miles! You can hike along parts of the wall, including some stretches near Beijing. Now this is a place for a selfie!

The Temple of Heaven

Doesn't this building look like it's reaching for the sky? It's the Hall of Prayer for Good Harvests, part of the Temple of Heaven complex, or 天坛 (Tiāntán). Chinese emperors came here to pray to the heavens for bountiful crops. Nowadays, the Temple of Heaven Park is a popular place to stroll or fly kites.

The Forbidden City

In China, the Forbidden City is generally called 故宫 (Gùgōng), literally "former palace." This compound of buildings is located in the heart of Beijing, and Chinese emperors lived and worked here from the early 1400s to the early 1900s.

By the Numbers

故宫 was dubbed "forbidden" because during imperial times most everyday people weren't allowed to enter. Today this site is open to the public and houses a museum that displays important objects from China's past. Here are some interesting facts about 故宫!

Has 980 buildings with over **8,700** rooms

Welcomed over **456 million** visitors from 1949 to 2019

Has over **1.8 million** artifacts in its museum collection

Source: The Palace Museum, 2020; Beijing Daily, 2020

REFLECT ON THE ESSENTIAL QUESTION

If you had a chance to take a trip, how would you decide what to see, eat, and do?

1 Would you want to visit popular sites or seek out lesser-known spots? Why?

2 What do you consider a must-see attraction in your state or country? Why?

3 If you were to visit Beijing, what would you want to visit or do? Why?

Discussing tourist attractions

1a Language Model TARGET LANGUAGE INPUT

Your teacher will lead a discussion about the images below. Try to participate as much as you can. If there is anything you don't understand, let your teacher know.

Běijīng yǒu shénme yǒuyìsi de jǐngdiǎn?

北京 - 有 - 什么 - 有意思 - 的 - 景点?

What interesting attractions are (there) in Beijing?

1

Chángchéng

长城

the Great Wall

2

Gùgōng

故宫

the Forbidden City

3

Tiāntán

天坛

Temple of Heaven

1b New Words in Context INTERPRETIVE

Listen to the audio and try to understand as much as you can. Then read the passage, using the pinyin text and vocabulary list to figure out unfamiliar words.

我朋友这个星期在北京。这个星期一她和她的
爸爸妈妈去了长城。他们这个星期二去了天坛。
昨天我和他们去了故宫。今天早上她问我：
"北京还有什么有意思的景点？"

Wǒ péngyou zhège xīngqī zài Běijīng. Zhège xīngqīyī tā hé tā de

bàba māma qù le Chángchéng. Tāmen zhège xīngqī'èr qù le Tiāntán.

Zuótiān wǒ hé tāmen qù le Gùgōng. Jīntiān zǎoshàng tā wèn wǒ:

"Běijīng hái yǒu shénme yǒuyìsi de jǐngdiǎn?"

Comprehension Check

		T	F
1	Sanjay's friend is in Beijing this week.	○	○
2	Sanjay went to visit the Great Wall with his friend.	○	○
3	Sanjay went to the Forbidden City with his friend and her parents, but he did not go with them to the Temple of Heaven.	○	○
4	Sanjay's friend knows exactly what she wants to do and see for the rest of her time in Beijing.	○	○

Vocabulary

Audio

	Word	Pinyin	Meaning
1	长城	Chángchéng	the Great Wall
2	天坛	Tiāntán	Temple of Heaven
3	故宫	Gùgōng	the Forbidden City
4	景点	jǐngdiǎn	tourist attraction/site, scenic spot

Complete the exercises below to check your understanding of what you reviewed in Section 1. If you have questions, consult the Language Review section.

Exercise 1 Read the Chinese sentences, then choose the better of the two English translations.

1 北京有很多很好的饭馆。

(a) There are many good restaurants in Beijing.

(b) Restaurants in Beijing have a lot of good food.

2 那个饭馆现在有人吗？

(a) Does that restaurant have any people?

(b) Is there anyone at that restaurant now?

Exercise 2 Rearrange the Chinese words and phrases in each row to translate the English sentences.

1 的 ｜ 昨天他 ｜ 买 ｜ 了 ｜ 一 ｜ 好看 ｜ 衣服。｜ 件

He bought a nice-looking piece of clothing yesterday.

2 我 ｜ 本 ｜ 一 ｜ 简单 ｜ 买 ｜ 想 ｜ 中文书。｜ 的

I want to buy a simple Chinese book.

Language Review

1 Using 有 to describe what can be found in an area

When used to describe a certain location, 有 can be translated either as "to have" or as "there is/ there are." 有 describes what can be found at a location, while 在 is used to say where something is.

1 北京有很多有意思的景点。

There are many interesting tourist attractions in Beijing. / Beijing has many interesting tourist attractions.

2 这个景点在北京。

This tourist attraction is in Beijing.

3 那个书店有很多中文书。

There are many Chinese books at that bookstore. / That bookstore has many Chinese books.

4 我们小区有一个篮球场，还有一个网球场。

There is a basketball court and a tennis court in our neighborhood. / Our neighborhood has a basketball court and a tennis court.

2 Using 的 in descriptions

When describing a noun in Chinese, the descriptive words, bolded below, will usually be connected to the noun with the character 的. One exception is that a single syllable adjective can generally be used without 的.

1 她想去一个有意思的景点。
_{jǐngdiǎn}

She wants to go to an interesting tourist site.

2 我昨天给她做了好吃的中国菜。

I made tasty Chinese food for her yesterday.

3 我和他是好朋友。

He and I are good friends.

What a Character!

土 (tǔ)

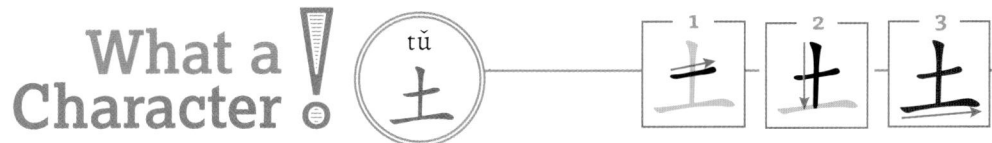

The component 土 (tǔ) means "earth." Characters containing this component often have to do with earth or soil.

For example, 城 (chéng) means "city wall, city" and early city walls in China were sometimes made from packed soil. Below are some characters that also contain the 土 (tǔ) component. What do they mean?

1 墙 (qiáng)

2 塔 (tǎ)

3 土地 (tǔdì)

1d Using the Language

What makes you want to visit a tourist site?

Step 1: Read the travel reviews that follow to help you choose two places you'd want to visit.

Step 2: In groups, tell your classmates where you want to go, making sure to mention what piece of information in the review led to that decision.

Step 3: Record your classmates' destination choices and reasons. What was the most common reason for wanting to visit a place? What was the least common reason?

Ming_818: 故宫有很多猫！我很喜欢猫，所以我很喜欢去故宫！故宫还有很多书和中国乐器。我觉得很有意思。可是周末故宫有很多人……

Lilyliu: 我这个周末去天坛了，那儿的人不太多。我给我朋友买了很多很好看的礼物。那儿还有一个饭馆，可是我觉得那个饭馆的菜不太好吃。

Traveller9: 长城这儿有很多饭馆，还有北京烤鸭！这儿的烤鸭很好吃！可是我不太喜欢做运动，所以我觉得去长城没有意思。

Small restaurants near the Great Wall

LANGUAGE CHALLENGE

长 (cháng) and 城 (chéng) mean "long" and "city, city wall" respectively in Chinese. If 城墙 (chéngqiáng) means "city wall," can you guess roughly what this tongue twister means?

长城长，城墙长，长长长城长城墙，城墙长长城长长。

Giving a strong opinion

2a Language Model TARGET LANGUAGE INPUT

Your teacher will lead a discussion about the image below. Try to participate as much as you can. If there is anything you don't understand, let your teacher know.

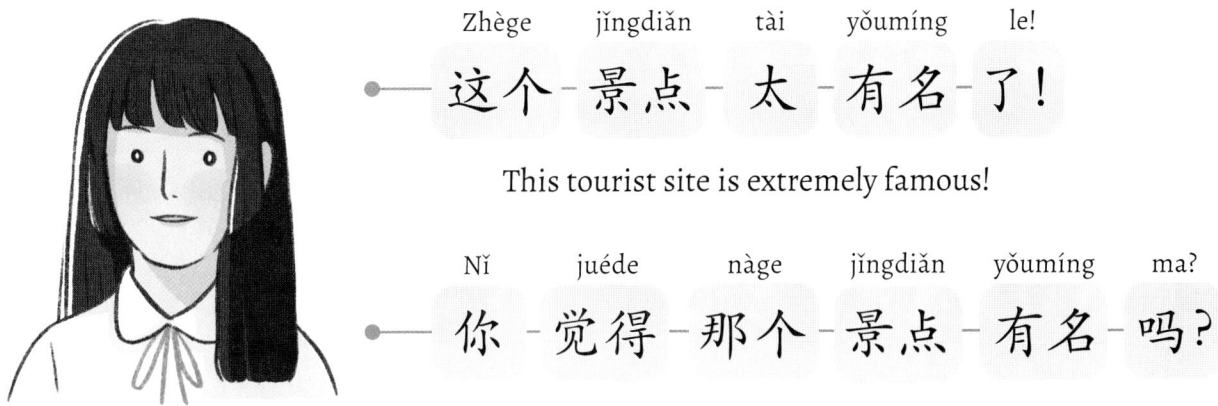

Zhège	jǐngdiǎn	tài	yǒumíng	le!
这个	景点	太	有名	了!

This tourist site is extremely famous!

Nǐ	juéde	nàge	jǐngdiǎn	yǒumíng	ma?
你	觉得	那个	景点	有名	吗?

Do you think that tourist site is famous?

2b New Words in Conversation INTERPRETIVE

Listen to the audio and try to understand as much as you can. Then read the dialogue, using the pinyin text and vocabulary list to figure out unfamiliar words.

 我们明天去那个景点吧？ Wǒmen míngtiān qù nàge jǐngdiǎn ba?

 那个景点太无聊了…… Nàge jǐngdiǎn **tài wúliáo** le...

 是啊，我也觉得那儿 Shì a, wǒ yě juéde nàr
不好玩儿。 bù **hǎowánr**.

 可是那个景点太有名了！ Kěshi nàge jǐngdiǎn **tài yǒumíng** le!
所以我很想去那儿…… Suǒyǐ wǒ hěn xiǎng qù nàr...

 好吧。那我们明天去 Hǎo ba. Nà wǒmen míngtiān qù
那儿。 nàr.

Comprehension Check

		T	F
1	Miko suggests that they go to a tourist site today.	○	○
2	Ellen and Leo think it's a fun place to go.	○	○
3	Miko, Ellen, and Leo decide to go to the tourist site together.	○	○

Vocabulary

	Word	Pinyin	Meaning
5	太	tài	too, extremely, overly
6	无聊	wúliáo	boring, bored
7	好玩儿	hǎowánr	fun
8	有名	yǒumíng	famous, well-known

Complete the exercise below to check your understanding of what you learned in Section 2.
If you have questions, consult the Language Reference section.

Rearrange the Chinese words and phrases in each row to translate the English sentences.

1 好玩儿 | 太 | 这 | 了! | 个 | 景点
This tourist site is a lot of (extremely) fun!

2 这 | 了! | 个 | 好 | 太 | 主意
This idea is great!

3 了。| 看 | 无聊 | 太 | 网球 | 觉得 | 我 | 比赛
I think watching tennis matches is extremely boring.

Language Reference

1 Expressing a strong feeling with 太...了

The pattern 太 (tài)...了 is used to express a strong feeling about something. It can be used to show excitement or to complain about something. 太 (tài)...了 communicates a stronger emotion than 很.

　　　　 tài
1 这本书太贵了。
This book is too expensive.

　　 tài
2 故宫太有意思了!
The Forbidden City is so interesting!

　　　　　　 tài wúliáo
3 他觉得那个电影太无聊了。
He thinks that movie is extremely boring.

　 tài
4 我太喜欢这个颜色了!
I love this color so much!

2d Using the Language   INTERPERSONAL

Can you guess your partner's opinions of the four places shown below? On a separate piece of paper, write down your prediction of whether your partner thinks each tourist attraction is famous, fun, interesting, or boring. After you finish making your guesses, ask your partner questions to see if your predictions were correct.

Example question:

你觉得这个景点有名吗？

1 *Tourists at Universal Studios in Singapore*

2 *The Statue of Liberty in New York, USA*

3 *Tourists river boating in Guilin, China*

4 *Tourists at the Louvre Museum in Paris, France*

5Cs

COMPARISONS

COMMUNITIES
COMMUNICATION
CULTURES
CONNECTIONS

Many Chinese words are created by combining two separate words. You've learned about some descriptive words that include 好, like 好吃 or 好听. Adjectives can also be formed by adding 有 before another word. Here are some examples:

$$有 + 名气 = 有名$$

míngqi

to have + fame, reputation = famous, well-known

$$有 + 用 = 有用$$

yòng   yǒuyòng

to have + to use = useful

$$有 + 劲 = 有劲$$

jìn   yǒujìn

to have + strength = strong

By contrast, descriptive words can be created in English by adding endings to words. For example, adding -ful to "use" creates the adjective "useful."

Use the Chinese words above to describe these images.

CHAPTER 2 Put the Pieces Together!

Audio

A Reading and Listening INTERPRETIVE

Passage 1

DAMING, ISABELLA, AND MARTIN ARE WALKING IN THEIR NEIGHBORHOOD.

Comprehension Check ✓

		T	F
1	Daming invites Martin and Isabella to go to a famous restaurant with him.	◯	◯
2	Martin doesn't like visiting famous tourist spots because they are too expensive.	◯	◯
3	Martin and Isabella both thought the Forbidden City was fun.	◯	◯
4	Isabella and Martin will go to the Great Wall with Daming and his friends this weekend.	◯	◯

Passage 2 Look at this map of Beijing tourist attractions. What do the red stars mean? Can you find the Great Wall, the Forbidden City, and the Temple of Heaven on this map?

Passage 3 Listen to the conversation. Answer the questions on a separate piece of paper.

1 What does the boy suggest doing in his neighborhood?
 (a) watching a soccer game
 (b) playing soccer
 (c) playing ping-pong

2 What does the girl think of the boy's suggestion?
 (a) fun
 (b) boring
 (c) interesting

3 What do they plan to do this afternoon?
 (a) play basketball
 (b) watch a good American movie
 (c) watch a famous Chinese movie

Passage 4 Listen to the conversation between the man and the woman. On a separate piece of paper, write which day thcy plan to visit cach tourist attraction.

Imagine that your class is working with a travel agency to develop interesting and educational student trips to Beijing. The agency wants to know your opinions, since you are their target market! Your teacher will assign one person in each group to act as the agency's market research interviewer and another student to take notes. The interviewer will ask the others in the group which of the places below they want (or don't want) to visit and why. (Reminder: Use 太 … 了 if you have a strong opinion about a place.) The notetaker will keep track of everyone's opinions and then report the top three choices. He/she will present these three destinations as a proposed itinerary for a trip around Beijing.

A bookstore in Beijing

The Great Wall of China

A clothing store in Beijing

Chefs working at Quanjude, Beijing's famous roast duck restaurant

The Temple of Heaven

A musical instrument store in Beijing

A lioness statue at the Forbidden City

Final Project PRESENTATIONAL

Create a Story

Jim (Chinese name: 小米) just spent a few days in Beijing. In pairs, write a story about his trip based on the images shown below. Make sure to include Jim's opinions on the things he did and the places he visited. Feel free to discuss the images in any order and to add details not shown in the pictures. Try to use 太 ⋯ 了 at least once.

Talk with your teacher if you have questions or if you are not certain you can do the following tasks:

- Name some famous Beijing tourist attractions and understand their importance, both historically and for the people of China today

- Understand descriptions of tourist attractions

- Tell others your opinions of different tourist attractions

- Express strong opinions

Cultural Knowledge

What did you learn about some Beijing tourist sites?

Let's Go!

Isabella: I can't wait to finally visit the Great Wall!

Martin: It seems like it will be a long bus ride to get there, though.

Daming: It'll be worth it. The Great Wall is really amazing!

Isabella: Besides, we can chat with Owen and Maya on the bus, so the ride won't be boring.

Martin: That's true! I wonder what Beijing sites they've already been to?

Isabella: We'll have to ask!

Can-Do Goals

In this chapter, you will learn to:

- Recognize some famous sites and events in China
- Discuss activities that are allowed (or not allowed) in certain locations
- Describe events that are fun to attend
- Understand and make comparisons

shènghuì   hé   jiéqìng

盛会和节庆
Events and Festivals

Travelers often plan their trips around fun and interesting
events, such as festivals and competitions. China hosts
events that draw crowds from all over the world.

Women's 110M hurdles at the 2008 Summer Olympics in Beijing

Beijing Olympics

Nearly 7 million sports fans
bought tickets for the Beijing
Summer Olympics, or 奥运会
(Àoyùnhùi), and the venues
are still an important tourist
draw. Beijing also won the
honor of hosting the 2022
Winter Olympics, making it the
first city in the world to host
both the Summer and
the Winter Olympics.

Harbin Snow & Ice Festival

For hearty travelers unafraid of
teeth-chattering cold, the city of
Harbin in northeastern China puts
on a festival featuring giant ice and
snow structures that visitors can
admire, walk through, and even climb
on. Each year, more than 10 million
attendees bundle up to see some of
the world's biggest ice sculptures,
many of which are lit up at night.
Travelers need to time their trip right,
though, because it's all gone by March.

Music Festivals

Love music? China has an abundance of music festivals to choose from featuring styles from classical to electronica. These people are attending one of China's biggest rock concerts, the Midi Music Festival. Different cities in China, including Beijing, Shanghai, and Shenzhen, have hosted this festival.

By the Numbers

The number of music festivals in China has shot up in recent years, giving music fans another reason to visit China.

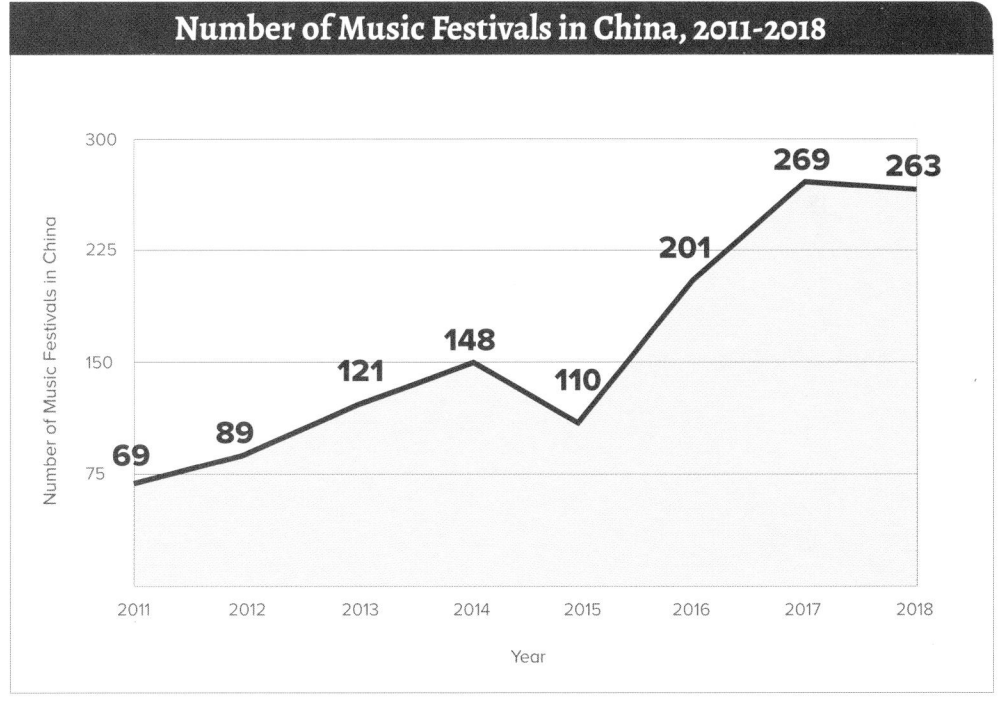

Number of Music Festivals in China, 2011-2018

Number of Music Festivals in China

69 · 89 · 121 · 148 · 110 · 201 · 269 · 263

2011 · 2012 · 2013 · 2014 · 2015 · 2016 · 2017 · 2018

Year

Source: Small Antlers Think Tank, Music Business China, 2019

REFLECT ON THE ESSENTIAL QUESTION

If you had a chance to take a trip, how would you decide what to see, eat, and do?

1 If you went to China, would you want to explore a current interest or try something new? Why?

2 Is your state or country known for a special event or festival? Do you think Beijing might have a similar event or festival?

3 Going to a big event means there will be crowds. Would the people make the event more enjoyable for you, or less?

Beijing Olympic attractions

1a Language Model TARGET LANGUAGE INPUT

Your teacher will lead a discussion about the images below. Try to participate as much as you can. If there's anything you don't understand, let your teacher know.

(handwritten note: J.O. Friday OH Chapter 3 Section 1 2 sentences (rearrange) to translation)

yóu yǒng	ma?
游泳	吗?

May I swim at the Water Cube?

Shuǐlìfāng

水立方

the Water Cube

The Water Cube is an aquatics center that was built for the 2008 Summer Olympics in Beijing. After the Olympics, an indoor water park was added, so now people can go there to swim and have fun!

Niǎocháo

鸟巢

the Bird's Nest

The Bird's Nest, named for its unusual architecture, is a stadium constructed for the Olympics that has a track and a soccer field. It is now used as a venue for concerts, sports matches, and more.

1b New Words in Conversation INTERPRETIVE

Listen to the audio and try to understand as much as you can. Then read the dialogue, using the pinyin text and vocabulary list to figure out unfamiliar words.

 我朋友这个周末想去
水立方和鸟巢。我不
知道我要不要去……
这两个景点好玩儿吗？

Wǒ péngyou zhège zhōumò xiǎng qù Shuǐlìfāng hé Niǎocháo. Wǒ bù zhīdào wǒ yào bú yào qù... Zhè liǎng gè jǐngdiǎn hǎowánr ma?

 好玩儿啊！你会游泳吗？
你可以去水立方游泳。

Hǎowánr a! Nǐ huì yóu yǒng ma? Nǐ kěyǐ qù Shuǐlìfāng yóu yǒng.

 我不太会游泳……
我喜欢踢足球和跑步！
我可以去鸟巢踢足球吗？

Wǒ bú tài huì yóu yǒng... Wǒ xǐhuan tī zúqiú hé pǎo bù! Wǒ kěyǐ qù Niǎocháo tī zúqiú ma?

 不可以……

Bù kěyǐ...

Comprehension Check

		T	F
1	Owen asks Miko if she knows where the Water Cube is.	○	○
2	Owen is very good at swimming and soccer.	○	○
3	Miko tells Owen that he can play soccer at the Bird's Nest.	○	○

Vocabulary

	Word	Pinyin	Meaning
1	水立方	Shuǐlìfāng	the Water Cube
2	鸟巢	Niǎocháo	the Bird's Nest
3	游泳	yóu yǒng	to swim; swimming
4	跑步	pǎo bù	to go running; running

Audio

1c Puzzle It Out PROGRESS CHECK

Complete the exercise below to check your understanding of what you reviewed in Section 1. If you have questions, consult the Language Review section.

Which word should be added to the following sentences? Choose 会 or 可以.

会 可以

1 她 ___ 游泳。
She knows how to swim.

○ ○

2 我哥哥不太 ___ 做菜。
My older brother can't really cook.

○ ○

3 你 ___ 给我弹吉他吗?
Could you play the guitar for me?

○ ○

4 你 ___ 去运动场跑步。
You can go running at the sports stadium.

○ ○

Language Review

1 可以 vs. 会

Although both 会 and 可以 are often translated as "can," the two words do not have the same meaning. 会 is used to talk about things you have learned how to do, and 可以 refers to things you are permitted to do or that the situation allows you to do.

yóu yǒng

1 他不会游泳。
He doesn't know how to (can't) swim.

2 你不可以在我家踢足球。
You're not allowed to (can't) play soccer at my house.

3 我会做菜。
I know how to (can) cook.

4 我明天可以给你打电话吗?
May (can) I call you tomorrow?

5 他很会弹古筝。
He knows how to (can) play the guzheng well.

6 你不可以在这儿弹吉他。
You're not allowed to (can't) play the guitar here.

1d Using the Language INTERPERSONAL / PRESENTATIONAL

In pairs, work together to create a dialogue based on the images below.

Step 1: Create a character and write at least three sentences that describe your character's interests. (Your partner will do the same for a character of his/her own.) Don't forget to name your character!

Step 2: Talk to your partner about what you can't do in each of the locations shown below.

Step 3: With your partner, create a dialogue between your two characters in which they discuss their shared interests, where they want to go, and when they have time to get together. Use the locations in the images for ideas.

What a Character!

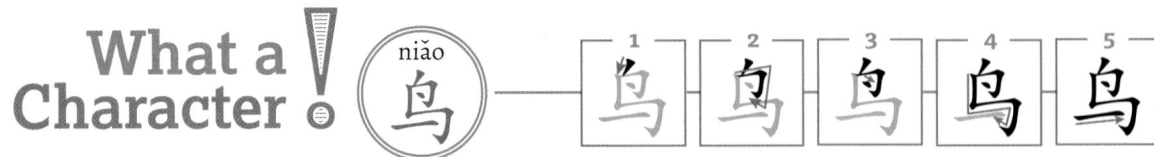

niǎo 鸟 — 鸟¹ 鸟² 鸟³ 鸟⁴ 鸟⁵

The character 鸟 (niǎo), which means "bird," sometimes appears as a component in the names of different types of birds.

You've already learned the character for "duck," 鸭 (yā). Which of the characters below do you think refer to other types of birds?

1 鸡   2 鹭   3 屿   4 玛   5 鹰   6 鹅

5Cs
COMMUNITIES
CONNECTIONS
COMMUNICATION
CULTURES
COMPARISONS

You've learned how to say the names of a few sports, and you also know how to cheer people on in Chinese! Make a poster in Chinese to support one of your school's sports teams. Here's an example:

游泳队
加油！

The word 队 (duì) means "team." Which team would you like to cheer for?

Comparing things

2a Language Model | TARGET LANGUAGE INPUT

Your teacher will lead a discussion about the image below. Try to participate as much as you can. If there is anything you don't understand, let your teacher know.

Àoyùnhuì	bǐ	yīnyuè	jié	yǒuyìsi	ma?
奥运会	比	音乐	节	有意思	吗?

Are the Olympic Games more interesting than a music festival?

The Olympic rings in Beijing

1

Àoyùnhuì

奥运会

the Olympic Games

2b New Words in Context INTERPRETIVE

Listen to the audio and try to understand as much as you can. Then read the passage, using the pinyin text and vocabulary list to figure out unfamiliar words.

我和我姐姐都很喜欢做运动，所以我们都很
喜欢看奥运会比赛。我姐姐还很喜欢听音乐。
这个周末她去了一个音乐节，她觉得去音乐节
比看比赛更有意思。我没有去音乐节，我去了
一个电影节，因为我觉得电影节一定比音乐节
好玩儿！

Wǒ hé wǒ jiějie dōu hěn xǐhuan zuò yùndòng, suǒyǐ wǒmen dōu hěn

xǐhuan kàn Àoyùnhuì bǐsài. Wǒ jiějie hái hěn xǐhuan tīng yīnyuè.

Zhège zhōumò tā qù le yí gè yīnyuè jié, tā juéde qù yīnyuè jié

bǐ kàn bǐsài gèng yǒuyìsi. Wǒ méiyǒu qù yīnyuè jié, wǒ qù le

yí gè diànyǐng jié, yīnwèi wǒ juéde diànyǐng jié yídìng bǐ yīnyuè jié

hǎowánr!

Comprehension Check

		T	F
1	Ellen and her sister like watching the Olympics.	○	○
2	Ellen went to a film festival this weekend but thinks that a music festival would be more fun.	○	○

Vocabulary

	Word	Pinyin	Meaning
5	奥运会	Àoyùnhuì	the Olympic Games
6	节	jié	festival, holiday
7	比	bǐ	compared with
8	更	gèng	even more

2c Puzzle It Out PROGRESS CHECK

Complete the exercise below to check your understanding of what you learned in Section 2. If you have questions, consult the Language Reference section.

Rearrange the Chinese words and phrases in each row to translate the English sentences.

1 难。 | 游泳 | 比 | 跑步
   Swimming is more difficult than running.

2 那件 | 好看。 | 衣服 | 这件 | 比 | 衣服
   This piece of clothing is nicer looking than that piece of clothing.

3 我妈妈 | 比 | 面条 | 更 | 好吃。 | 觉得 | 饺子
   My mom thinks that noodles are even tastier than dumplings.

Language Reference

1 Using 比 and 更 to make comparisons

The word 比 (bǐ) is used to compare two things. In English, we often say "X is more [descriptive word] than Y," but in Chinese, the structure is "X 比 (bǐ) Y [descriptive word]."

1 这本书比那本书贵。

This book is more expensive than that book.

2 我觉得包子比饺子好吃。

I think baozi are tastier than dumplings.

更 (gèng) can be added before a descriptive word to emphasize that something is even more [descriptive word] than something else.

3 我觉得包子比饺子更好吃！

I think baozi are even tastier than dumplings!

4 故宫比天坛更有名！

The Forbidden City is even more famous than the Temple of Heaven!

If what is being compared is clear, 更 (gèng) can be used on its own and, in these cases, 更 (gèng) means "even more" or just "more."

5 我觉得饺子很好吃，可是面条更(gèng)好吃。

   I think dumplings are really tasty, but noodles are (even) tastier.

6 马丁很喜欢拉二胡。春月觉得弹古筝更(gèng)有意思。

   Martin likes playing the erhu. Isabella thinks playing the guzheng is more interesting.

2d Using the Language INTERPERSONAL

Work with a partner and compare the pairs of images. Keep track of your partner's responses and be ready to discuss his/her opinions to the rest of the class.

Example:

A: 你觉得电影节比音乐节更好玩儿吗？

B: 对！我喜欢看电影，所以我觉得电影节比音乐节好玩儿。

有名：	故宫		长城 
无聊：	跑步		做菜 
有意思：	打篮球		游泳 

LANGUAGE CHALLENGE

节 means "festival" or "holiday," and is used in the names of different holidays, including the important Chinese holiday Spring Festival (春节). Look up the names of other festivals or holidays that use the character 节. Here are a couple of hints:

Put the Pieces Together!

 Audio

A Reading and Listening INTERPRETIVE

Passage 1

DAMING, ISABELLA, MARTIN, OWEN, AND MAYA ARE ON A BUS ON THEIR WAY TO THE GREAT WALL.

1 北京太好玩儿了！

是啊！
你们去了什么好玩儿的景点？

2 我去了故宫和天坛。

3 我也去了这两个景点！
我还去了鸟巢和水立方。

我经常去水立方游泳，
所以我觉得水立方比鸟巢好玩儿。

4 你很喜欢游泳吗？

很喜欢！
我还很喜欢听音乐，所以
下个星期我要去北京音乐节。

5 北京有音乐节？

对啊！

那北京有电影节吗？

Comprehension Check

		T	F
1	Both Owen and Maya have visited the Forbidden City and the Temple of Heaven.	○	○
2	Maya thinks the Water Cube is more fun than the Bird's Nest.	○	○
3	There is a roast duck festival in China.	○	○
4	They will probably have hot pot for lunch.	○	○

Passage 2 This river in China has a sign stating some things that are not allowed. According to the sign, what is one activity that you cannot do here?

Passage 3 Listen to the conversation between the man and the woman, then answer the following questions.

1 Why does the man want to go to the U.S. in June?
  (a) to go to a famous film festival
  (b) to watch basketball games
  (c) to visit famous tourist sites

2 Why does the woman want to go to the U.S. in April?
  (a) to go to a film festival
  (b) to go to a music festival
  (c) to watch the Olympic Games

3 The man and the woman ultimately decide to visit the U.S. in which month?
  (a) January
  (b) April
  (c) June

4 Which activity do they both want to do?
  (a) watch a basketball game
  (b) watch a swimming competition
  (c) go to a music festival

Passage 4 Listen to the boy talk about different kinds of sports, then rank the sports shown below according to his preferences, from the one he likes the best to the one he likes the least.

A B C D

B Speaking INTERPERSONAL

Look at the pictures below and compare the different events. Which two events do you want to go to, and which two are you less interested in? In pairs, compare the different events. Does your partner have the same opinions as you? Be prepared to share your own and your partner's comparisons of the different events with the class.

A

Dogs at a pet festival in Kyiv, Ukraine

B

A ramen noodle festival in Yamanashi, Japan

C

The Ultra Music Festival in Miami, Florida, United States

D

The Olympic Rings in Paris, France

Sports Commentator

Imagine that you are a sportscaster covering the Summer Olympics in Beijing. Working in groups, decide if you will comment on a running event or a swimming event. With help from your teacher, find a brief video clip from the 2008 Beijing Olympics. Then work with your group mates to write a simple script about that competition. Try to include the following in your commentary:

- Where you are right now (the location of the competition)
- The name of the person (or people) you're focusing on
- The nationality of the person you're focusing on
- How fast or slow that person is compared to others in the competition (see the Word Bank for additional words)
- Whether that person won or not (see the Word Bank for additional words)

Remember that you can cheer the competitors on! Once your script is complete, practice saying it along with the video. Be prepared to present your clip to the class!

WORD BANK

kuài	màn	yíng	shū
1 快	**2** 慢	**3** 赢	**4** 输
fast	slow	to win	to lose

Can-Do Goals

Talk with your teacher if you have questions or if you are not certain you can do the following tasks:

- Recognize some famous sites and events in China
- Discuss activities that are allowed (or not allowed) in certain locations
- Describe events that are fun to attend
- Understand and make comparisons

Cultural Knowledge

What are some events that people might travel to China for?

Ice structures and sculptures in Harbin, Heilongjiang Province

SCHOOL LIFE

In Unit 2, you will learn to talk about classes, time, and how you are feeling. You will also learn to talk about favorites and express mild opinions.

Essential Question
How is student life similar throughout the world?

A school building in Heihe, Heilongjiang Province

CHAPTER 4
Too Many Classes!

Martin is struggling to choose courses and turns to Isabella for help.

CHAPTER 5
How's It Going?

Martin emails Daming and tells him about the challenges of adjusting to a new school.

CHAPTER 6
Taking Care of Yourself

Emma and Isabella convince Martin, who has a fever, to stay home from school.

At the end of the unit, you will imagine that students from your sister school in China are planning a visit as exchange students, and they have questions about what your school is like. You will:

- Read a letter in which one of the Chinese students tells you about his/her school life and asks questions about your school experience

- Work in pairs to share information from the Chinese students' letters and discuss how their school is the same as or different from yours

- Write a letter to the Chinese students comparing your schools and answering specific questions from their letters

Too Many Classes!

Martin: Isabella, have you seen the list of courses our new school offers? There are so many interesting classes!

Isabella: I've taken a look at it. I think I've figured out what I want to take.

Martin: Really?! That quickly!

Isabella: Yeah, it was pretty simple.

Martin: I guess I need to spend more time thinking about it...

Can-Do Goals

In this chapter, you will learn to:

- Understand the Chinese school system and compare it to your own
- Talk about your favorite classes
- Tell someone what you are about to do
- Express mild opinions
- Describe someone's feelings

xuéyè   xuǎnzé

学业选择

Educational Choices

In China, students must complete six years of primary school (grades 1–6) and three years of middle school (grades 7–9). High school is an additional three years of study, and although it is not mandatory, most Chinese students take advantage of the opportunity to go to high school. While this basic structure is consistent across the nation, differences between schools and in the choices that individual Chinese students make result in a unique school experience for every student.

Many students, such as these in a Beijing high school, stay in the same classroom most of the day while different teachers come in to teach their various subjects.

By the Numbers

Academic vs. Vocational

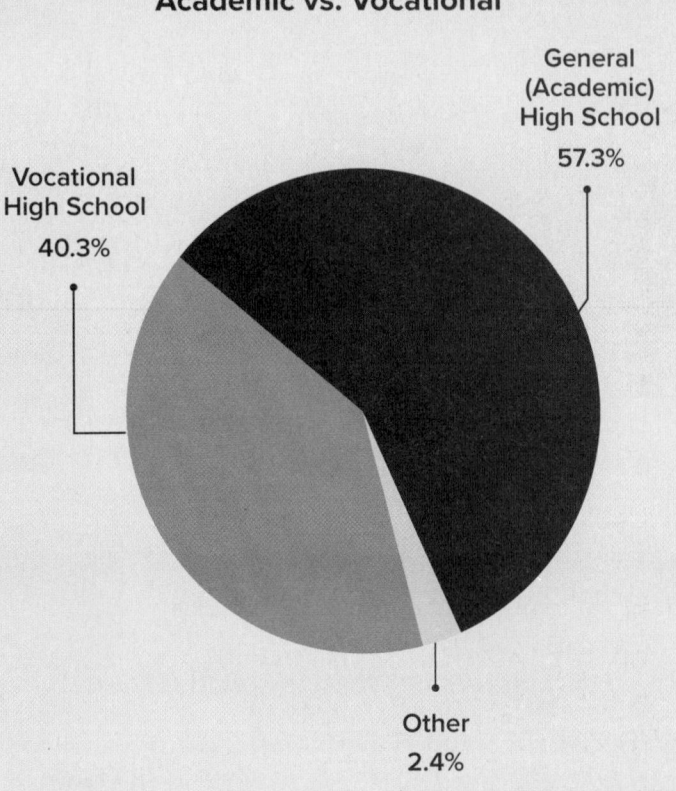

General (Academic) High School
57.3%

Vocational High School
40.3%

Other
2.4%

Source: Ministry of Education, People's Republic of China, 2018

Taking Different Paths After Middle School

Students take a major exam at the end of middle school. How well they do on this exam determines whether they can enter a general (academic) school or a vocational school. A small number of students make the choice to stop attending school altogether. This chart shows the percentage of students enrolled in the two types of high school in 2018.

A lively English class in Zhejiang Province

Standard Subjects

Unlike Martin and Isabella, who go to an international school, most students in Chinese public schools don't get much say in what classes they take except in the last two years of high school. Students typically study Chinese, math, a foreign language (usually English), social studies, science, and physical education.

A Chance to Choose Courses

Recently, the Chinese government has called for more electives as part of an effort to increase creativity, interaction, and individuality in the education system. In some general high schools, 11th and 12th grade students now get to mix in electives with their required courses.

REFLECT ON THE ESSENTIAL QUESTION

How is student life similar throughout the world?

1 What courses are required at your school? Do you think those requirements make sense?

2 How much choice do Chinese students typically have in their coursework compared with how much you have?

3 Choosing to go onto high school is a major decision for young Chinese people. Have you ever made a choice that made a major difference in your life?

Class preferences

1a Language Model TARGET LANGUAGE INPUT

Your teacher will lead a discussion about the images below. Try to participate as much as you can. If there is anything you don't understand, let your teacher know.

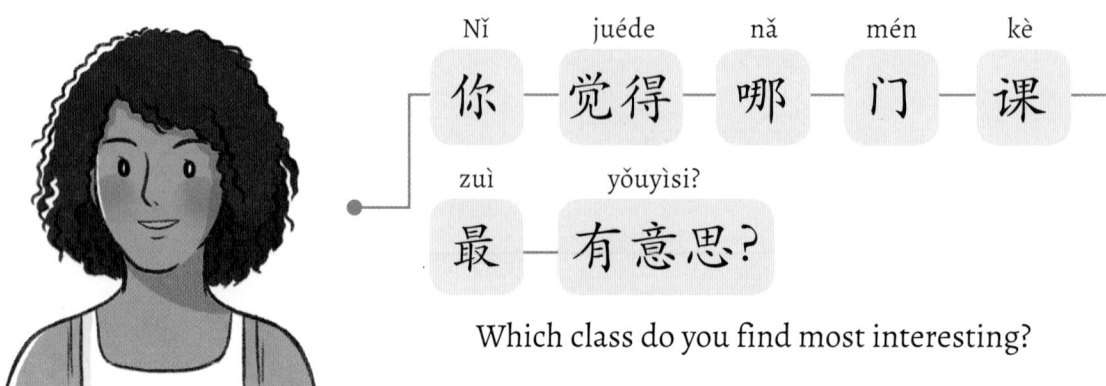

Nǐ	juéde	nǎ	mén	kè
你	觉得	哪	门	课

zuì	yǒuyìsi?
最	有意思?

Which class do you find most interesting?

1

shùxué

数学

math

2

kēxué

科学

science

Audio

School is now in session. Listen as Maya and Sanjay discuss their classes, and try to understand as much as you can. Then read the dialogue, using the pinyin text and vocabulary list to figure out unfamiliar words.

 你最喜欢哪门课？

Nǐ zuì xǐhuan nǎ mén kè?

 我最喜欢科学课。你呢？

Wǒ zuì xǐhuan kēxué kè. Nǐ ne?

 我也最喜欢科学课。
我觉得科学课最有意思。
我还很喜欢数学课。

Wǒ yě zuì xǐhuan kēxué kè.

Wǒ juéde kēxué kè zuì yǒuyìsi.

Wǒ hái hěn xǐhuan shùxué kè.

Comprehension Check ✓

		T	F
1	Maya asks Sanjay which class he likes the most.	◯	◯
2	Sanjay's favorite class is music.	◯	◯

Vocabulary

Audio

	Word	**Pinyin**	**Meaning**
1	最	zuì	most, -est
2	哪	nǎ	which
3	门	mén	(measure word for a course)
4	课	kè	course, class, lesson
5	科学	kēxué	science
6	数学	shùxué	math

LANGUAGE CHALLENGE

You may have noticed that many subject names in Chinese end with the character 学. In some of these cases, you can think of 学 as meaning "the study of ___." Here are some subjects that end with 学. Can you guess which subjects they refer to?

jīngjì
经济 + 学 = 经济学
economy + 学 = ?

shēngwù
生物 + 学 = 生物学
living things + 学 = ?

shèhuì
社会 + 学 = 社会学
society + 学 = ?

zhé
哲 + 学 = 哲学
wise + 学 = ?

1c Puzzle It Out PROGRESS CHECK

Complete the exercise below to check your understanding of what you learned in Section 1. If you have questions, consult the Language Reference section.

Use the words in the list on the left to complete each sentence below. Use each word once.

哪
哪儿
那
那儿

1 你最喜欢 ___ 只宠物?
2 我们去 ___ 个乐器店吧!
3 你们现在在 ___ ?
4 ___ 有一个乒乓球馆。

Language Reference

1 Using 哪 to ask which

When asking a question that would include "which" in English, use 哪 (nǎ). 哪 (nǎ) should always be followed by a measure word, as shown in bold below.

1 你想学^{nǎ}哪种乐器？

Which instrument do you want to learn?

2 他^{zuì}最想买^{nǎ}哪本书？

Which book does he want to buy the most?

If it is already clear what is being talked about, sometimes the noun after 哪 (nǎ) can be left out, but the measure word still needs to be included. In these cases, 哪 + a measure word means something like "which one."

3 这三^{mén}门^{kè}课都很有意思。你觉得^{nǎ mén zuì}哪门最有意思？

These three classes are all very interesting. Which one do you think is most interesting?

1d Using the Language INTERPERSONAL

In an international survey, blue was the most common favorite color in many countries, including the United States, China, and Germany.[1] But is it the most common favorite color in your class?

Step 1: In groups, discuss your classmates' favorite colors. Keep track of the answers and be prepared to report back to your teacher.

Step 2: Have one student tell the teacher the favorite colors of the others in his/her group.

Step 3: After each group has shared the results, figure out what the most common favorite color in your class is!

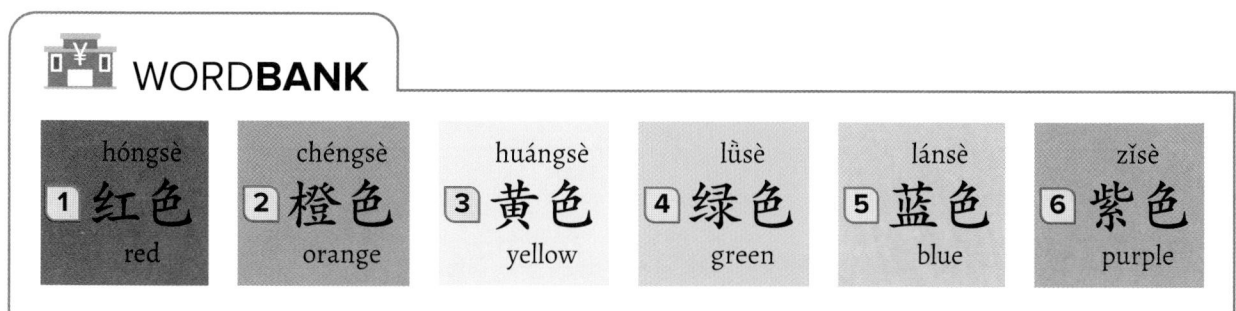

WORD**BANK**

hóngsè	chéngsè	huángsè	lǜsè	lánsè	zǐsè
1 红色	2 橙色	3 黄色	4 绿色	5 蓝色	6 紫色
red	orange	yellow	green	blue	purple

[1] Source: YouGov.com

Choosing courses

2a Language Model   TARGET LANGUAGE INPUT

Your teacher will lead a discussion about the image below. Try to participate as much as you can. If there is anything you don't understand, let your teacher know.

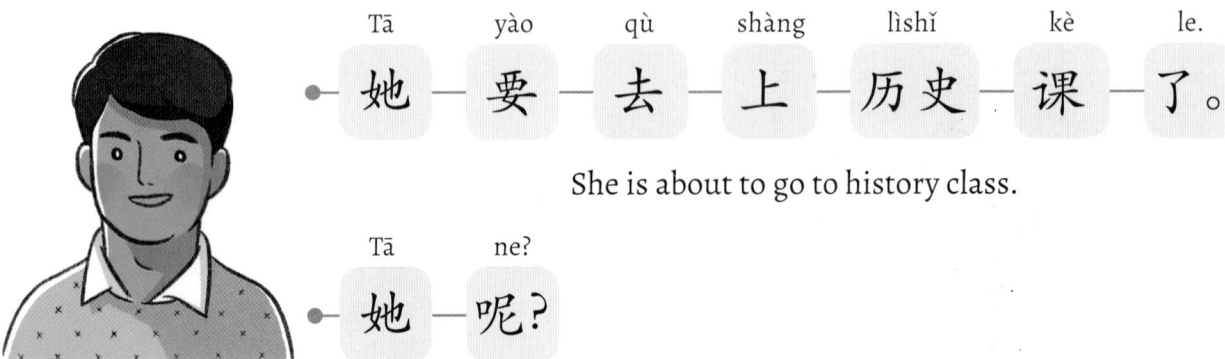

Tā	yào	qù	shàng	lìshǐ	kè	le.
她	要	去	上	历史	课	了。

She is about to go to history class.

Tā	ne?
她	呢?

What about her?

1	2
lìshǐ	wénxué
历史	文学
history	literature

Listen to the audio and try to understand as much as you can. Then read the dialogue, using the pinyin text and vocabulary list to figure out unfamiliar words.

 你选了历史课还是美国文学课？

Nǐ xuǎn le lìshǐ kè háishi Měiguó wénxué kè?

 我朋友说历史课比美国文学课更重要，所以我选了历史课。你呢？

Wǒ péngyou shuō lìshǐ kè bǐ Měiguó wénxué kè gèng zhòngyào, suǒyǐ wǒ xuǎn le lìshǐ kè. Nǐ ne?

 我选了美国文学课，因为我觉得文学课比历史课有意思！我要去上课了……再见！

Wǒ xuǎn le Měiguó wénxué kè, yīnwèi wǒ juéde wénxué kè bǐ lìshǐ kè yǒuyìsi! Wǒ yào qù shàng kè le... Zàijiàn!

 好，我也要去上课了，再见！

Hǎo, wǒ yě yào qù shàng kè le, zàijiàn!

Comprehension Check

		T	F
1	Owen asks if Ellen likes history or American literature.	○	○
2	Ellen chose history class because she thinks literature is boring.	○	○

Vocabulary

	Word	Pinyin	Meaning
7	选	xuǎn	to choose
8	历史	lìshǐ	history
9	文学	wénxué	literature
10	说	shuō	to say, to speak

Audio

	Word	Pinyin	Meaning
11	重要	zhòngyào	important
12	上课	shàng kè	to go to a class, to begin a class, to be in class

5Cs CULTURES

COMMUNITIES
COMMUNICATION
CONNECTIONS
COMPARISONS

In China, class often begins with the teacher saying "上课 (shàng kè)" to indicate that class is starting. After the teacher announces that class is starting, students are usually expected to stand and greet the teacher with "老师好!"

A teacher instructing her class in Hebei Province

2c Puzzle It Out   PROGRESS CHECK

Complete the exercise below to check your understanding of what you learned in Section 2. If you have questions, consult the Language Reference section.

Choose the sentences that indicate that something is about to happen.

1. 我们要去看篮球比赛了。
2. 她买了一本很好看的书。
3. 他们要去上课了。
4. 她后天要给我打电话。

Language Reference

2 Expressing that something is about to happen with 要...了

The word 要 (to be going to) can be paired with 了 to talk about something that is about to happen.

1 她要去打网球了。 She's about to go play tennis.

2 他们要去看电影了。 They're about to go see a movie.

3 我现在要做菜了。 I'm going to cook now.

2d Using the Language INTERPERSONAL

Activity 1 Write a sentence in Chinese describing something that someone is about to do. Then, turn the paper over and draw a picture to illustrate the sentence that you wrote. Give your drawing to your teacher, who will hang all the pictures around the classroom. With a partner, look at your classmates' pictures and discuss what you think the person in each picture is about to do. Take notes and prepare to discuss your ideas with the class.

Activity 2 In general, would the students in your class rather learn about science or history?

Step 1: In groups, use Chinese to discuss your opinions about science and history. Ask which subject is more interesting, more important, and more difficult.

Example: 你觉得科学比历史重要吗？为什么？

Step 2: After everyone in the group has given their opinions, have one student tell the teacher how many students have each opinion. Is your class full of history buffs or science nerds?

Talking about feelings

3a Language Model TARGET LANGUAGE INPUT

Your teacher will lead a discussion about the image below. Try to participate as much as you can. If there is anything you don't understand, let your teacher know.

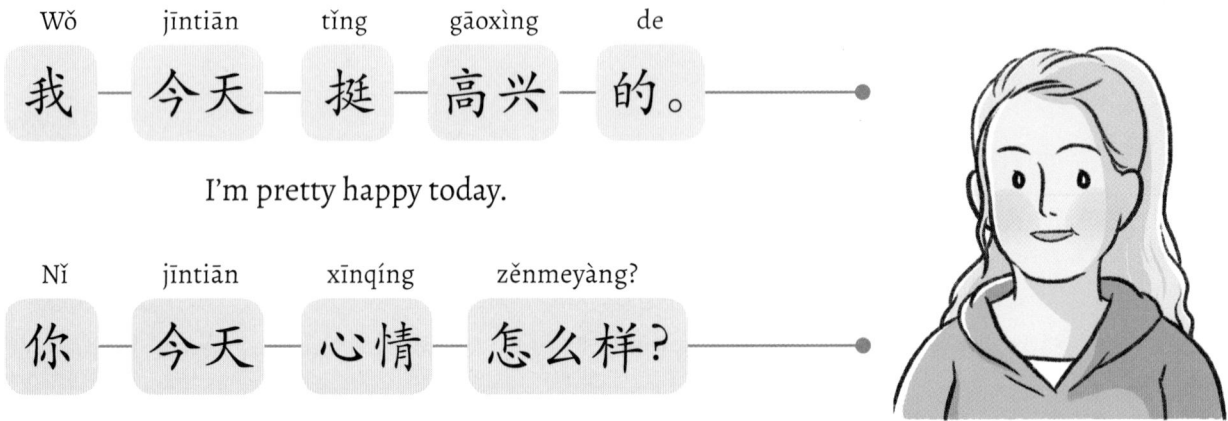

Wǒ jīntiān tǐng gāoxìng de
我 — 今天 — 挺 — 高兴 — 的。

I'm pretty happy today.

Nǐ jīntiān xīnqíng zěnmeyàng?
你 — 今天 — 心情 — 怎么样?

How are you feeling (emotionally) today?

3b New Words in Conversation INTERPRETIVE

Listen to the conversation Miko, Owen, and Sanjay are having just before Owen and Sanjay's soccer match and try to understand as much as you can. Then read the dialogue, using the pinyin text and vocabulary list to figure out unfamiliar words.

 你们现在心情怎么样？   Nǐmen xiànzài **xīnqíng zěnmeyàng**?

 我挺高兴的。   Wǒ **tǐng gāoxìng** de.

 我太紧张了。   Wǒ tài **jǐnzhāng** le!

 我去给你们加油吧，怎么样？   Wǒ qù gěi nǐmen jiā yóu ba, **zěnmeyàng**?

 好啊！   Hǎo a!

Comprehension Check

                     T   F

1 Owen is unhappy.   ○   ○

2 Sanjay is extremely nervous.   ○   ○

Vocabulary

Audio

	Word	Pinyin	Meaning
13	心情	xīnqíng	mood, state of mind
14	怎么样	zěnmeyàng	How is…? ; How about it? Is it OK? How does that sound?
15	挺	tǐng	quite, fairly, pretty, rather
16	高兴	gāoxìng	happy, pleased
17	紧张	jǐnzhāng	nervous, anxious

Complete the exercise below to check your understanding of what you learned in Section 3. If you have questions, consult the Language Reference section.

Use the words in the list to the left to complete each sentence below. Use each word once.

了
的
挺
太

1 这个菜 ⬚⬚ 好吃了！

2 我觉得红烧肉 ⬚⬚ 好吃的。

3 历史课太有意思 ⬚⬚ ！

4 这门课挺难 ⬚⬚ 。

Language Reference

3 Using 挺 … 的 to indicate degree

Like 太 … 了, the pattern 挺 (tǐng) … 的 shows how much the speaker feels a certain way. 太 … 了 indicates a stronger feeling than 挺 (tǐng) … 的.

   tǐng   gāoxìng
1 我今天挺高兴的。   I'm fairly happy today.

⚠️ **TAKE NOTE**

> 快乐 and 高兴 (gāoxìng) both mean "happy," but they are used differently. 高兴 (gāoxìng) is used to describe more everyday emotions and cannot be used to wish someone a happy birthday or a happy holiday. 快乐 is somewhat formal and is often used to describe longer stretches of time (like a happy childhood), as well as to wish a happy birthday.

       tǐng
2 这本书挺贵的。   This book is pretty expensive.

3 那门课 挺^(tǐng) 难 的。   That course is fairly difficult.

4 这种音乐 挺^(tǐng) 好听 的。   This type of music is quite pleasant.

5 他 挺^(tǐng) 喜欢做运动 的。   He quite likes exercising.

What a Character!

青 (qīng)

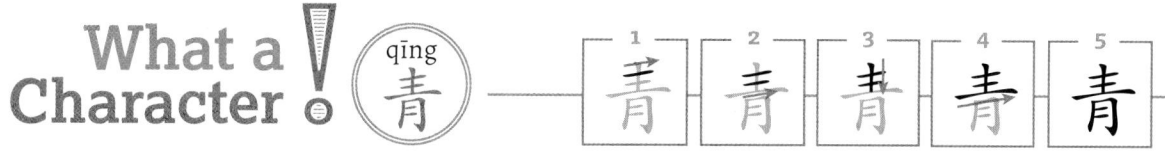

Characters with the component 青 are frequently pronounced "qing" or "jing." The component 青 is often found on the right side of a character.

Practice saying the three words below. Based on previous knowledge of components, can you match each word to its meaning?

1 清 (qīng)   **2** 晴 (qíng)   **3** 友情 (yǒuqíng)

a friendship

b clear, pure

c sunny, clear

3d Using the Language   INTERPERSONAL

In this activity, you and your classmates will pretend to be one of the four people below. Your task is to ask your partner about his/her emotions from Sunday through Wednesday and try to guess which person he/she is pretending to be. The first person to guess correctly wins, and if you guess incorrectly, you automatically lose!

Example:

A: 你星期二心情怎么样？

B: 我星期二挺高兴的。

	星期天	星期一	星期二	星期三
大史				
心月				
小文				
星科				

Put the Pieces Together!

A Reading and Listening INTERPRETIVE

Audio

Passage 1

MARTIN'S ANXIETY ABOUT GOING TO A NEW SCHOOL SHOWS AS HE STRUGGLES TO CHOOSE HIS CLASSES.

Comprehension Check

		T	F
1	Martin is not in a great mood because he is having difficulty choosing classes.	○	○
2	Martin has already chosen a science class and a history class.	○	○
3	Isabella thinks that the science class is easy, but the history class is extremely difficult.	○	○
4	Isabella is about to go play ping-pong, but Martin continues talking to her.	○	○

Passage 2 Your friend recently bought this shirt because she liked the design. But she doesn't know Chinese and wants to know what it means! What does the writing say?

Passage 3 Listen to the conversation and answer the questions on a separate piece of paper.

1 What does Ellen say about science class?

   (a) She also thinks science class is difficult.
   (b) She quite likes going to science class.
   (c) She thinks science class is pretty boring.

2 Which class does Ellen think is more difficult than science class?

   (a) American literature
   (b) history
   (c) math

3 Which subject is most interesting to Leo?

   (a) history
   (b) Chinese
   (c) math

B Speaking INTERPERSONAL

Imagine that your school library plans to expand its collection of history books. Below are some books being considered. (Hint: Chinese uses abbreviations in situations. For example, 历史 can be abbreviated as 史 in book titles.) In groups, tell your classmates which two books you want to read and why you think they are a better choice compared to the other two books. After discussing your group mates' preferences and reasons, agree on two books as a group. Then explain your choices to the class.

C Final Project PRESENTATIONAL

Class Selection

A Chinese student is planning to come study at your school! His name is 明明, and he has written a few notes to the class and is hoping you can find ways to help him in his studies.

Step 1: Read the note, paying attention to the subjects 明明 might need help in.

Step 2: Talk to your classmates to learn who thinks those subjects are interesting and who is willing to teach them to the exchange student.

Step 3: Write back to 明明 and tell him which classes you like and which are easy for you. Also tell 明明 which students can tutor him if he has trouble with any of his classes.

我觉得英文课和数学课很难!

I think english and math are very hard

我最喜欢上历史课,我最不喜欢上科学课。

favorite class is history   least favorite is science

你最喜欢什么课? 你觉得哪门课最好学?

Your favorite class is what?   Which class do you think is the best

Can-Do Goals

Talk with your teacher if you have questions or if you are not certain you can do the following tasks:

- Understand the Chinese school system and compare it to your own
- Talk about your favorite classes
- Tell someone what you are about to do
- Express mild opinions
- Describe someone's feelings

Cultural Knowledge

What did you learn about China's school system?

Students studying in their classroom in Jiangxi Province

How's It Going?

Emma: So guys, how is school going so far?

Isabella: It's going great! I really like my classmates, and the teachers are alright.

Martin: It's going okay, I guess. . . .

Emma: Yeah? I'd love to hear more!

Martin: I'm pretty tired. I'll be in my room — let me know when dinner's ready.

Can-Do Goals

In this chapter, you will learn to:

- Discuss the specific time of an activity or event

- Understand when others talk about running later than expected

- Talk about what you need to do every day or every week

- Talk about doing things with other people

- Express how you are the same as or different from someone else

- Understand aspects of student life in China and compare them to your own experience

xuéshēng   shēnghuó

学生生活

Student Life

Ask students anywhere in the world whether they're busy, and the answer will likely be a resounding "yes!" Here's what middle and high school in China often looks like.

Long Days

Secondary-school classes in China generally begin around 8:00 a.m. and go until 5:00 p.m. or later. There's a midday break, which often lasts about two hours, to give students a chance to eat lunch, nap, and recharge.

Students in Chengdu, Sichuan Province enjoy lunch outside their school.

Studying as a Group

Chinese students, such as the Beijing high school students shown here, largely stay with the same classmates throughout the day and spend a lot of time studying as a group. During the morning period before classes begin, students in middle school (grades 7–9) and high school (grades 10–12) study or read books aloud together. At many high schools, students must also return to school after dinner to study together—which makes for a long day!

Cram Schools

In addition to going to school, many students attend evening and weekend "cram schools," or 补习班 (bǔxíbān), to prepare for high school and college entrance exams. The scores earned on these tests largely determine which high schools and colleges students can get into, so pressure to do well can be intense.

12th graders in Chengdu, Sichuan Province enter a test site for the college entrance exam.

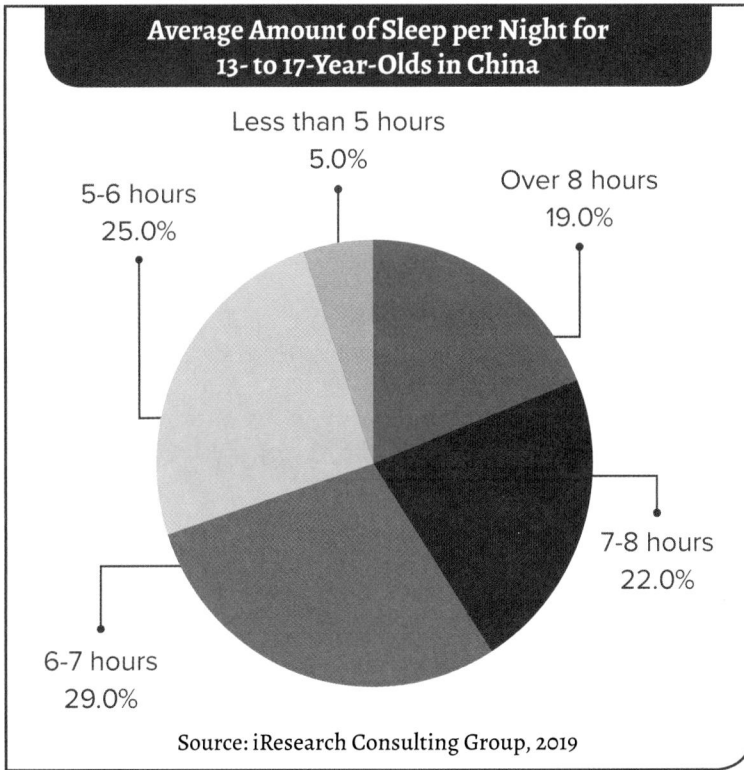

Average Amount of Sleep per Night for 13- to 17-Year-Olds in China

Less than 5 hours
5.0%

Over 8 hours
19.0%

5-6 hours
25.0%

7-8 hours
22.0%

6-7 hours
29.0%

Source: iResearch Consulting Group, 2019

By the Numbers

Between school, studying, and cram schools, teens in China often get less than the recommended 8–10 hours of sleep.

In an online survey of Chinese students and their parents, "too much homework" was the most common reason given for not getting enough sleep.

REFLECT ON THE ESSENTIAL QUESTION

How is student life similar throughout the world?

1. How does school life in China compare with your school experience? What are the similarities and differences?

2. Do you need to take standardized tests? What are they for, and how do you prepare for them?

3. If you could change something about your school and study schedule, what would you change? Why?

Talking about time

1a Language Model TARGET LANGUAGE INPUT

Your teacher will lead a discussion about the images below. Try to participate as much as you can. If there is anything you don't understand, let your teacher know.

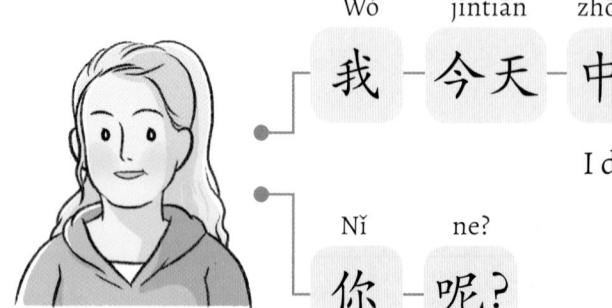

Wǒ jīntiān zhōngwǔ shí'èr diǎn cái qǐ chuáng.
我 今天 中午 十二 点 才 起床。

I didn't get up until noon today.

Nǐ ne?
你 呢?

How about you?

qǐ chuáng
1 起床
to get up

shuì jiào
2 睡觉
to sleep

zuò zuòyè
3 做作业
to do homework

1b New Words in Context `INTERPRETIVE`

Audio

Listen to the audio and try to understand as much as you can. Then read the passage, using the pinyin text and vocabulary list to figure out unfamiliar words.

昨天晚上七点我去看篮球比赛了。比赛很好看！可是我晚上九点十分才开始做作业，十一点半才睡觉。我今天早上六点二十分才起床。下个星期我们学校还有篮球比赛。我去不去看呢？

Zuótiān wǎnshàng qī diǎn wǒ qù kàn lánqiú bǐsài le. Bǐsài hěn hǎokàn!
Kěshì wǒ wǎnshàng jiǔ diǎn shí fēn cái kāishǐ zuò zuòyè, shíyī diǎn bàn
cái shuì jiào. Wǒ jīntiān zǎoshàng liù diǎn èrshí fēn cái qǐ chuáng. Xià gè
xīngqī wǒmen xuéxiào hái yǒu lánqiú bǐsài. Wǒ qù bú qù kàn ne?

Comprehension Check

		T	F
1	Leo didn't start doing his homework until 9:10 p.m. last night.	○	○
2	He went to bed at 10:30 p.m.	○	○

Vocabulary

Audio

	Word	Pinyin	Meaning
1	点	diǎn	o'clock (literally, dot or point)
2	分	fēn	minute
3	才	cái	not until, only then
4	开始	kāishǐ	to start, to begin; beginning
5	作业	zuòyè	homework
6	半	bàn	half, half an hour
7	睡觉	shuì jiào	to sleep
8	起床	qǐ chuáng	to get up, to get out of bed

1c Puzzle It Out PROGRESS CHECK

Complete the exercises below to check your understanding of what you learned in Section 1.
If you have questions, consult the Language Reference section.

Exercise 1 Match the times shown in Chinese to the times shown on the clocks.

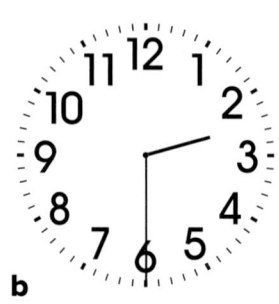

1 六点四十二   **2** 两点半   **3** 十二点十分

Exercise 2 Rearrange the Chinese words and phrases in each row to translate the English.

1 半 | 七 | 早上 | 点
7:30 a.m.

2 下午 | 今天 | 分 | 四 | 二十五 | 点
4:25 this afternoon

3 我 | 十点 | 起床。 | 半 | 才
I didn't wake up until 10:30.

4 才 | 点 | 六 | 分 | 开始。 | 十八 | 比赛 | 篮球
The basketball game didn't start until 6:18.

5 开始 | 九点 | 她昨天 | 看 | 才 | 晚上 | 那本 | 书。
She didn't start reading that book until 9 p.m. last night.

Language Reference

1 The basics of telling time

When giving the time, the time of day (if provided) is stated first, followed by the hour, and then the minutes.

Time of day (optional)	Hour	点 (diǎn)	Minutes*	分** (fēn)	Meaning
1	八	点	五	分	8:05
2 早上	六	点	十	分	6:10 a.m.
3	八	点	○五	（分）	8:05
4	七	点	十八	（分）	7:18
5 晚上	十	点	二十四	（分）	10:24 p.m.
6	五	点			5:00
7	三	点	半 (bàn)		3:30 p.m. (literally, three hours and a half)
8	几	点?			At what time [will something happen]?

*For minutes less than ten, you can add ○ (líng), which means "zero," before the number of minutes.

** 分 (fēn) can be omitted when the number of minutes is more than one character. 分 (fēn) is never used with 半 (bàn).

2 Expressing that something happened later than expected

才 (cái) means "not until" or "only then." It is added after a time phrase to express that the action that follows happened later than expected or desired. 了 is not used with 才 (cái), even when talking about completed actions.

1 我昨天去给她买礼物了。 I went and bought a gift for her yesterday.

2 我昨天才去给她买礼物。 (cái) I didn't go buy a gift for her until yesterday.

Studies have found that, in general, teenagers tend to be "night owls," often staying up late at night and waking up late in the morning. Is that the case for students in your class?

Step 1: Get into groups and conduct an interview circle. The teacher will select one student in each group to start the interview. Student 1 will ask the student to the right (student 2) when he/she went to sleep last night and woke up this morning. Student 2 will then interview the next student to the right. Continue in a circle until everyone in the group has been interviewed. Take note of the responses of everyone in your group. If you feel you went to sleep late or woke up late, remember to use 才 when giving your answer.

Example: 昨天晚上我十一点才睡觉。

Step 2: The teacher will call on one student from each group to report back. When do students in your class go to sleep and wake up? Do the results of this class survey support the idea that teens are night owls?

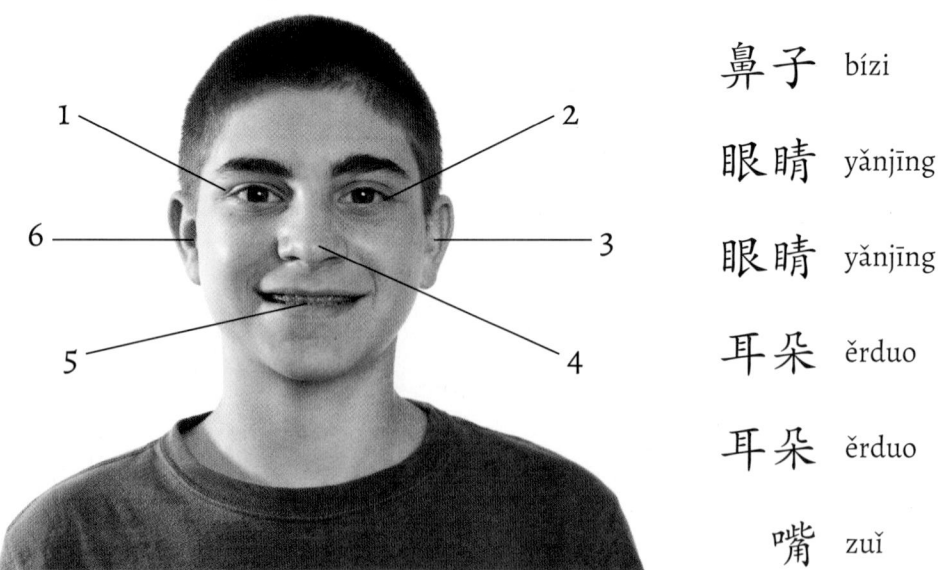

What a Character!

mù 目 — 目 目 目 目 目

The component 目 (mù) in 睡觉 (shuì jiào) means "eye" or "look." It usually appears on the left side or bottom of a character.

Take a look at the list of words for facial features. Which contain the component 目 (mù)? Which contain the component 口? With these clues, match the words to the features marked on the picture.

鼻子 bízi

眼睛 yǎnjīng

眼睛 yǎnjīng

耳朵 ěrduo

耳朵 ěrduo

嘴 zuǐ

Bonus Question: 眉毛 (méimao) is another facial feature. Can you guess what it means?

Talking about schedules

2a Language Model TARGET LANGUAGE INPUT

Your teacher will lead a discussion about the images below. Try to participate as much as you can. If there is anything you don't understand, let your teacher know.

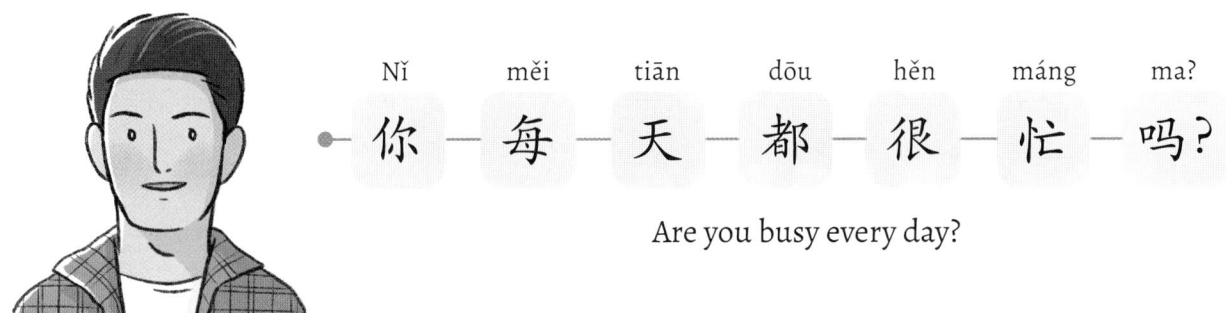

Nǐ	měi	tiān	dōu	hěn	máng	ma?
你	每	天	都	很	忙	吗?

Are you busy every day?

lèi

1 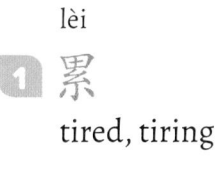 累
tired, tiring

máng

2 忙
busy

2b New Words in Conversation INTERPRETIVE

Listen to the audio and try to understand as much as you can. Then read the dialogue, using the pinyin text and vocabulary list to figure out unfamiliar words.

 你今天有时间踢足球吗？

Nǐ jīntiān yǒu **shíjiān** tī zúqiú ma?

没有。我很忙，我每天都
有很多课和很多作业······

Méiyǒu. Wǒ hěn **máng**, wǒ **měi tiān** dōu
yǒu hěn duō kè hé hěn duō zuòyè...

 那你周末想去踢足球吗？

Nà nǐ zhōumò xiǎng qù tī zúqiú ma?

我周末不用上课，可是
我得拉二胡、做作业。我
周末很累，不想踢足球。

Wǒ zhōumò **búyòng** shàng kè, kěshì
wǒ **děi** lā èrhú, zuò zuòyè. Wǒ
zhōumò hěn **lèi**, bù xiǎng tī zúqiú.

Comprehension Check

		T	F
1	Owen asks if Miko has time to play soccer today.	○	○
2	Miko says she has to play guzheng every day, so she is too busy.	○	○

Vocabulary

	Word	Pinyin	Meaning
9	时间	shíjiān	time
10	忙	máng	busy
11	每	měi	every, each
12	天	tiān	day
13	不用	búyòng	don't need to, don't have to
14	得	děi	must, to have to, need to
15	累	lèi	tired, tiring

5Cs

COMPARISONS

COMMUNITIES
COMMUNICATION
CONNECTIONS
CULTURES

There are certain things most Chinese students are required to do. Generally, Chinese students must learn a foreign language. (The most common choice is English.) Every morning, most students do group exercises together. And most schools have a flag-raising ceremony on Monday mornings attended by the whole student body.

Are there things that your school requires all students to do?

Students doing exercises in Xingtai City, Hebei Province

2c Puzzle It Out PROGRESS CHECK

Complete the exercise below to check your understanding of what you learned in Section 2. If you have questions, consult the Language Reference section.

Use the words in the list on the left to complete each sentence below. You will use each word twice.

每	1 我 ＿＿ 个星期五晚上 ＿＿ 去看电影。
都	2 爸爸说："你明天一定 ＿＿ 去。"
得	3 她 ＿＿ 天 ＿＿ 做作业。

3 Expressing "every" with 每...都

The structure 每 (měi) . . . 都 is used to describe what is true for every/each thing that you are talking about.

1 <ruby>每<rt>měi</rt></ruby>个人都有名字。   Everyone (every person) has a name.

2 他觉得<ruby>每<rt>měi</rt></ruby>门课都挺难的。   He thinks every course is quite difficult.

3 我<ruby>每天<rt>měi tiān</rt></ruby>都看电视。   I watch TV every day.

> ⚠️ **TAKE NOTE**
>
> 每 (měi) should always be followed by a measure word. Since 天 (tiān) acts as its own measure word, you should not add 个 (or any other measure word) before 天 (tiān).

4 Talking about what you have to do

A number of different Chinese verbs can be used to say that you "must" or "have to" do something. 要 is one, although it has a number of other meanings as well. 得 (děi) is also used to talk about things that you have to do or must do.

1 我<ruby>每天<rt>měi tiān</rt></ruby>都要做作业。
I need to do homework every day.

2 我星期天下午<ruby>得<rt>děi</rt></ruby>去中文学校。
I have to go to Chinese school on Sunday afternoons.

3 老师说，我们都<ruby>得<rt>děi</rt></ruby>看这本书。
The teacher said that we all have to read this book.

To express that someone does not have to do something, use 不用 (búyòng).

4 我这个星期^{búyòng}不用去中文学校。

I don't need to go to Chinese school this week.

5 老师说，我们^{búyòng}不用看这本书。

The teacher said that we don't have to read this book.

2d Using the Language INTERPERSONAL

Step 1: Select how busy you feel, on average, from the following options:

很忙 ｜ 挺忙的 ｜ 不太忙 ｜ 不忙

If you feel busy, write a sentence or two describing what you need to do every day or every week. If you don't feel so busy, describe the things you have time to do.

Examples:

我每天都很忙。我每天下午都得拉二胡，晚上还得做作业。OR

我不太忙，我每天都有时间听音乐和看电视。

Step 2: In groups, conduct an interview circle to learn whether your classmates feel busy every day or not. Take notes on what they say they need to do or have time to do. Be prepared to report back to the rest of the class.

Shared experiences

3a Language Model TARGET LANGUAGE INPUT

Your teacher will lead a discussion about the image below. Try to participate as much as you can. If there is anything you don't understand, let your teacher know.

Zhōngguó	cài	gēn	Měiguó	cài	yíyàng	hǎochī	ma?
中国	菜	跟	美国	菜	一样	好吃	吗?

Is Chinese food as tasty as American food?

Nǐ	xiǎng	gēn	wǒ	yìqǐ	qù	chī	fàn	ma?
你	想	跟	我	一起	去	吃	饭	吗?

Do you want to go eat with me?

Audio

Listen to Maya and Sanjay discuss where they want to eat and try to understand as much as you can. Then read the dialogue, using the pinyin text and vocabulary list to figure out unfamiliar words.

我有的时候喜欢吃中国菜，有的时候喜欢吃美国菜。你呢？

Wǒ yǒude shíhou xǐhuan chī Zhōngguó cài, yǒude shíhou xǐhuan chī Měiguó cài. Nǐ ne?

我跟你一样。我觉得中国菜跟美国菜一样好吃！

Wǒ gēn nǐ yíyàng. Wǒ juéde Zhōngguó cài gēn Měiguó cài yíyàng hǎochī!

春月跟我说，她很喜欢吃美国菜。我们跟她一起去美国饭馆吃饭吧？

Chūnyuè gēn wǒ shuō, tā hěn xǐhuan chī Měiguó cài. Wǒmen gēn tā yìqǐ qù Měiguó fànguǎn chī fàn ba?

可是她已经去吃饭了……

Kěshì tā yǐjīng qù chī fàn le ...

Comprehension Check

		T	F
1	Maya likes eating both Chinese and American food.	◯	◯
2	Sanjay doesn't really like American food.	◯	◯
3	Maya suggests going to an American restaurant with Isabella.	◯	◯
4	In the end, Sanjay, Isabella, and Maya all go out to eat together.	◯	◯

Vocabulary

	Word	Pinyin	Meaning
16	有的	yǒude	some
17	时候	shíhou	(a point in) time, moment
18	跟	gēn	with, and; to
19	一样	yíyàng	same, alike; as...as
20	一起	yìqǐ	together
21	已经	yǐjīng	already

3c Puzzle It Out PROGRESS CHECK

Complete the exercise below to check your understanding of what you learned in Section 3. If you have questions, consult the Language Reference section.

Use the words in the list on the left to complete each sentence below.

跟
一起
一样

1 她 ⬚ 她哥哥 ⬚ 去打篮球了。

2 我 ⬚ 他们不太 ⬚ 。

3 我 ⬚ 他说，我们可以明天去买衣服。

LANGUAGE CHALLENGE

When a word is made of two (or more) characters, the meaning of the word is often a combination of the meanings of the separate characters. Based on the characters you've learned, try to match each unfamiliar word to its meaning.

1 时区 (shíqū)
2 炒饭 (chǎofàn)
3 多样性 (duōyàngxìng)

a diversity   b time zone   c fried rice

Language Reference •

5 Talking about doing things with someone

When used as a linking word, 跟 (gēn) often means "with" or "and." Unlike the English "with," 跟 (gēn) must go between the two people or things being discussed and before the main action word in the sentence. In many cases, including the following sentences, 跟 (gēn) and 和 can be used interchangeably.

1 他跟他爸爸一起去了书店。
   gēn   yìqǐ

He went to the bookstore with his father.

2 她想跟她朋友去看电影。
          gēn

She wants to go see a movie with her friend.

跟 (gēn) can also mean "to" when it links a person doing an action to the person he/she is acting towards.

3 春月跟马丁说，"那个饭馆的菜不太好吃。"
        gēn

Isabella said to Martin, "That restaurant's food is not very tasty."

6 Saying things are the same or alike with 一样

X 跟 (gēn) Y 一样 (yíyàng) or X 和 Y 一样 (yíyàng) is used to say that two things or people are the same or alike.

1 我跟他一样。我们有的时候很忙，有的时候不太忙。
   gēn   yíyàng   yǒude shíhou   yǒude shíhou

He and I are just the same. Sometimes we're busy, sometimes we're not too busy.

> **! TAKE NOTE**
>
> 时候 (shíhou) and 时间 both refer to time, but they are used in different ways. 时间 refers to the idea of time or an amount of time, while 时候 (shíhou) talks about certain points in time.

To negate X 跟 (gēn) Y 一样 (yíyàng) or X 和 Y 一样 (yíyàng), simply add 不 in front of 一样 (yíyàng).

2 中国菜跟美国菜不一样。
 gēn   yíyàng

Chinese food and American food are not the same.

一样 (yíyàng) can also be used to say that one thing is "as [descriptive word] as" something else. When used this way, the structure is X 跟 (gēn) Y 一样 (yíyàng) [descriptive word].

3 这个周末我和你一样忙。
              yíyàng

I am as busy as you are this weekend.

4 历史课跟科学课一样难。
        gēn   yíyàng

History class is as difficult as science class.

3d Using the Language INTERPERSONAL

Talk about things that you have difficulty choosing between because they are equally enjoyable. Complete the sentences below based on your own experience and preferences. Ask your partner how he/she completed each sentence. Tell your partner if you agree or disagree, and prepare to discuss with the class.

课：＿＿＿北＿＿＿ 跟 ＿正艮＿＿＿ 一样有意思。

运动：＿网王木＿ 跟 ＿足王木＿ 一样有意思。

菜：＿中国木＿ 跟 ＿米国莫＿ 一样好吃。

比赛：＿门言弓木＿比赛跟 ＿网王木＿ 比赛一样有意思。

Put the Pieces Together!

A Reading and Listening INTERPRETIVE

Audio

Passage 1

MARTIN WRITES AN EMAIL TO DAMING, AND IT'S CLEAR THAT MARTING IS HAVING TROUBLE ADJUSTING TO HIS NEW SCHEDULE.

105

5

昨天是星期二。
我跟春月说：
"我今天晚上一定要九点睡觉！"

6

可是，我昨天晚上
很想拉二胡，所以
我八点半才开始做
作业。
我十一点十分才
睡觉……

7

今天早上我七点十分才起床。

8

我跟妈妈说：
"明天我一定要
六点半起床！"

9

今天早上我觉得很累，
可是在我们学校每个学生
早上都要做运动……

我很不喜欢早上做运动。
春月跟我不一样，
她觉得早上做运动很好。

106

Comprehension Check

		T	F
1	Martin is tired and anxious every day.	○	○
2	Martin plans to go to sleep at 10:30 every night.	○	○
3	On Tuesday night, Martin wanted to play the erhu.	○	○
4	This morning Martin woke up earlier than he expected, at 7:00 a.m.	○	○
5	Neither Martin nor Isabella likes exercising in the morning.	○	○

Passage 2 According to the mask, what is this woman doing?

我睡着了

Passage 3 Listen to Owen and Miko's conversation. Are the following statements true (T) or false (F)?

		T	F
1	Miko feels very tired.	○	○
2	Miko didn't have much homework last night.	○	○
3	Miko didn't go to bed until eleven o'clock last night.	○	○
4	Martin is tired, just like Miko.	○	○

B Speaking INTERPERSONAL

Think of a person you admire and write some notes in Chinese about that person's daily routine. You can imagine these details or do research to find out. Using your notes, tell a classmate about the person you have chosen. When does he/she get up in the morning and go to bed at night? What kinds of things does he/she have to do every day? Then listen as your partner tells you about the schedule of the person he/she selected. If these two people wanted to meet up, what time of day would they both be free?

C | Final Project | PRESENTATIONAL

Comparing Schedules

Step 1: Write your daily schedule for Friday and Saturday, including the specific times that you are doing things. Write 有事 if you don't know how to say an activity in Chinese.

Step 2: Read the schedule below, which shows what a Chinese student's schedule for Friday and Saturday might look like. (Students in China all have different schedules!) The asterisks show things that the student is required to do.

Step 3: Be prepared to answer the following questions in class.

- How is your schedule and this Chinese student's schedule the same? Do you both need to do some of the same things?

- Are there things you have to do that this student does not, or things this student has to do that you do not?

- Who is busier, you or the Chinese student?

星期五

6:30 a.m.	起床
6:50 a.m.	吃早饭
7:40 a.m.	跟同学一起在学校看书*
8:00 a.m.	上课*
10:15 a.m.	跟同学一起做运动*
12:00 p.m.	吃饭
12:30 p.m.	睡午觉
2:00 p.m.	上课*
5:50 p.m.	吃晚饭
6:25 p.m.	跟同学一起做作业
10:20 p.m.	睡觉

星期六

9:30 a.m.	起床
10:00 a.m.	去英文学校上课*
11:10 a.m.	在家上数学课*
12:30 p.m.	跟朋友去饭馆吃饭
2:00 p.m.	睡午觉
2:45 p.m.	拉二胡*
4:00 p.m.	踢足球*
6:00 p.m.	看电视
8:00 p.m.	在taobao.com买衣服
9:30 p.m.	听音乐
10:40 p.m.	睡觉

Can-Do Goals

Talk with your teacher if you have questions or if you are not certain you can do the following tasks:

- Discuss the specific time of an activity or event
- Understand when others talk about running later than expected
- Talk about what you need to do every day or every week
- Talk about doing things with other people
- Express how you are the same as or different from someone else
- Understand aspects of student life in China and compare them to your own experience

Cultural Knowledge

What does a typical Chinese school day look like?

A group of Beijing high school students in class

Taking Care of Yourself

Isabella: Hey Martin, want to watch a movie tonight?

Martin: Don't you have homework to do?

Isabella: I already finished! So, do you want to watch a movie?

Martin: I don't think I'll have time. I still have a lot of homework to do. And I'm feeling kind of run down, so I shouldn't stay up too late.

Isabella: Yeah, you don't look so good....

Can-Do Goals

In this chapter, you will learn to:

- Understand things Chinese students might do to stay healthy
- Talk about what you can do and what the situation allows you to do
- Discuss adjusting plans to do something a bit earlier or later
- Understand when others say they are hungry, thirsty, hot, or cold
- Talk about common health problems
- Express what you do (and do not do) when you are sick

111

xuéshēng   jiànkāng

学生健康
Student Health

You've probably heard the saying, "Prevention is the best medicine." Here are a few of the things Chinese students might do to stay well and to prevent health problems.

Keeping Hydrated...and Warm

What's in this thermos? In China, it is just as likely to be hot water as it is to be tea or coffee. Many Chinese drink hot or warm water, especially when they're not feeling well, because they believe that drinking hot water is better for one's body than drinking cold water. Schools often provide hot water dispensers to allow students to refill their thermoses throughout the day.

Annual Group Physicals

From elementary through high school, students across China get physical exams once a year to make sure they are in good health. Many schools do not have a school nurse, so healthcare workers may come to the school to conduct the physicals.

Eye Breaks

Pausing as a group to massage pressure points around the eyes is a daily routine in many Chinese schools. The exercise is meant to reduce eye fatigue and vision problems. Myopia (near-sightedness) is considered a major health concern, and the government has set targets to try to decrease the number of students who become myopic.

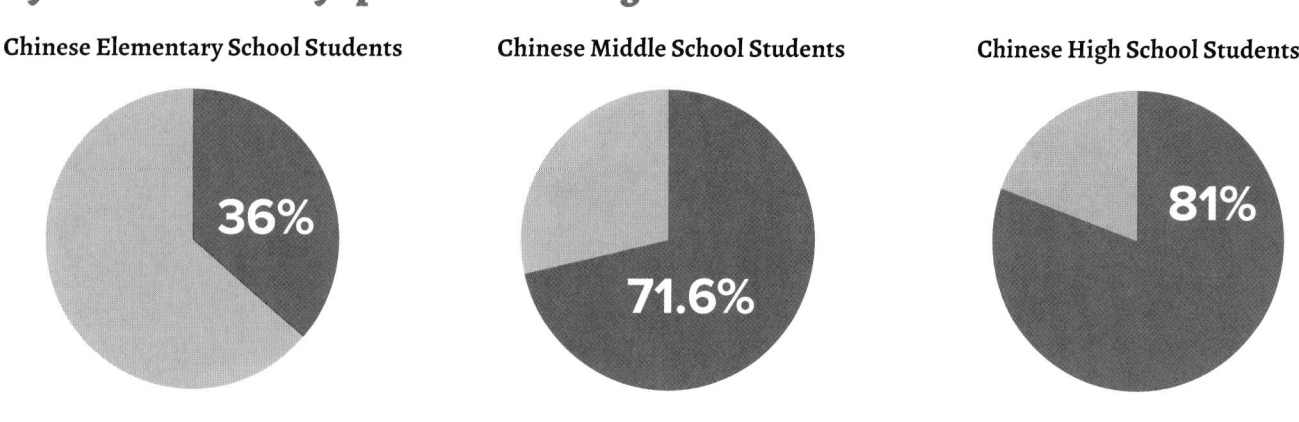

Students at a Shanghai high school take a break from classwork to do their eye exercises

By the Numbers: Myopia Rates Among Chinese Students

Chinese Elementary School Students

36%

Chinese Middle School Students

71.6%

Chinese High School Students

81%

Source: National Health Commission of the People's Republic of China, 2018

■ = Percentage of students with myopia

REFLECT ON THE ESSENTIAL QUESTION

How is student life similar throughout the world?

1 What do you do to take care of yourself when you are not feeling well? Would you try drinking hot or warm water? Why or why not?

2 Do you think eye exercises would be beneficial to you? Are there any exercises you do to stay healthy?

3 What health services or programs does your school offer?

Just a little bit

1a Language Model TARGET LANGUAGE INPUT

Your teacher will lead a discussion about the images below. Try to participate as much as you can. If there is anything you don't understand, let your teacher know.

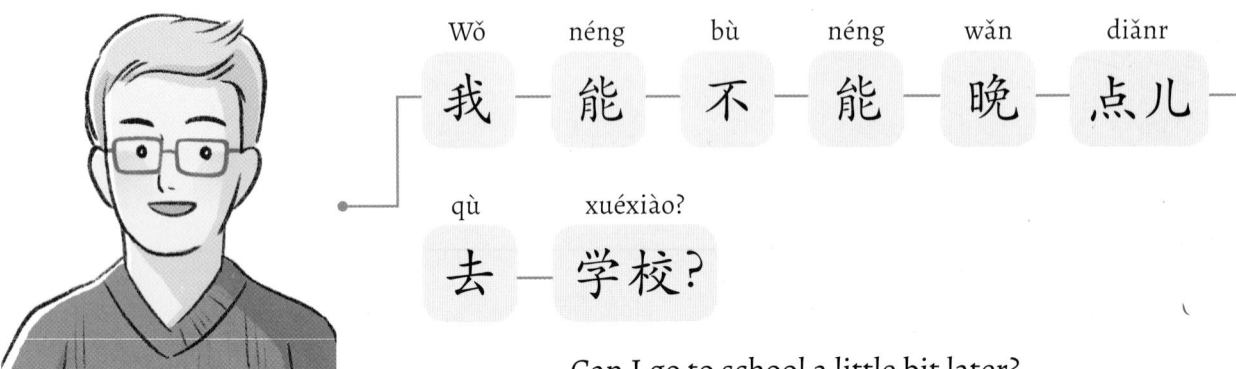

Wǒ néng bù néng wǎn diǎnr
我 — 能 — 不 — 能 — 晚 — 点儿

qù xuéxiào?
去 — 学校?

Can I go to school a little bit later?

wǎn
1 晚
late

zǎo
2 早
early

Audio

Listen to the audio and try to understand as much as you can. Then read the dialogue, using the pinyin text and vocabulary list to figure out unfamiliar words.

 爸爸，我觉得很累······
我今天能不能请假？

Bàba, wǒ juéde hěn lèi...
Wǒ jīntiān néng bù néng qǐng jià?

 不能。

Bù néng.

那我能晚一点儿去学校吗？

Nà wǒ néng wǎn yìdiǎnr qù xuéxiào ma?

 也不能。你喝点儿水，吃
点儿饭，早点儿去学校吧！

Yě bù néng. Nǐ hē diǎnr shuǐ, chī
diǎnr fàn, zǎo diǎnr qù xuéxiào ba!

多 a lot mǎy
土 / less /少少 le

Comprehension Check

T   F

1 Leo asks if he could take today off.   ◯ ◯

2 Leo's dad says that Leo can go to school a little later.   ◯ ◯

Vocabulary
Audio

	Word	Pinyin	Meaning
1	能	néng	can, to be able
2	请假	qǐng jià	to ask for time off, to ask to be excused from (school, work)
3	晚	wǎn	late
4	（一）点儿	(yì)diǎnr	a bit, a little, some
5	喝	hē	to drink
6	水	shuǐ	water
7	早	zǎo	early

Complete the exercise below to check your understanding of what you learned in Section 1. If you have questions, consult the Language Reference section.

Rearrange the Chinese words and phrases in each row to translate the English sentences.

1 点儿 | 我们 | 晚 | 能 | 去 | 不能 | 吃饭?

Can we go eat a little bit later?

我们

2 明天她 | 我们 | 不能 | 和 | 一起 | 看电影。 | 去   *together*

She can't go watch a movie with us tomorrow.

明天她不能 去 看 电影 和 我们一走

Language Reference

1 Stating what you are able to do with 能

能 (néng) expresses what you are capable of doing and what you are willing to do, but it can also be used when talking about what you are allowed to do.

1 她能吃二十个饺子。

néng

She can eat twenty dumplings.

néng   néng

2 你能不能跟我一起做这个菜?

Can you cook this dish with me?

néng   néng

3 妈妈，我能不能去看足球比赛?

Mom, can I go watch the soccer game?

In many cases, 能 (néng) and 可以 can be used interchangeably. 不能 (néng) is used more often when you are unwilling to do something or when the situation prevents you from doing something. By contrast, 不可以 gives more emphasis to the fact that you are not allowed to or do not have permission to do something.

néng

4 我明天没有空，不能跟你去看电影。

I don't have time tomorrow, so I can't go to the movies with you.

5 A: 你可以教我弹吉他吗?

Would you teach me how to play the guitar?

        néng
B: 不能!

No! (Nothing is preventing me from teaching you, but I am unwilling to do so.).

COMMUNITIES
COMMUNICATION
CONNECTIONS
CULTURES

There are regional differences in how all languages are spoken. In Chinese, one common variation is the addition of an "r" sound (儿) to the ends of some words. This even has its own name: 儿化音 (érhuàyīn). One example of 儿化音 (érhuàyīn) is 一点儿 (yìdiǎnr). In some parts of China, 一点 is pronounced yìdiǎn. But for many Chinese people, especially those in the north, it is pronounced 一点儿 (yìdiǎnr), which sounds like yìdiǎr, with the last syllable said in a nasal way. What are some regional accents in your country?

2 Expressing "a bit" with (一)点儿

（一）点儿 ([yì]diǎnr) is often used before a noun, and it means to "do a little bit of (that noun)," as shown below. The 一 in this phrase is usually optional.

           diǎnr
1 你去做点儿作业吧。   You should go do a bit of homework.

        yìdiǎnr
2 我能吃一点儿这个菜吗?   Can I have a bit of this dish?

When（一）点儿 ([yì]diǎnr) is used immediately after a descriptive word, it means "a bit more [descriptive word]."

3 今天我要早^{zǎo}点儿^{diǎnr}睡觉。 I am going to go to bed a bit earlier today.

（一）点儿 ([yì]diǎnr) can also be used to soften the tone, especially when making a suggestion.

4 喝^{Hē}点儿^{diǎnr}水^{shuǐ}。 Have some water.

5 喝^{Hē}水^{shuǐ}！ Drink the water!

1d Using the Language INTERPERSONAL

You played ping-pong with a friend this morning, and you had so much fun that you decided to spend the whole day together. Work in pairs, with one person using Schedule A and the other using Schedule B. Talk with your partner and see how many events you can do together. To be able to do more things together, you will need to ask your partner to do things earlier or later. Also, you will need to be willing to adjust your own schedule!

Example:

我们四点去看篮球比赛吧？……那你能早点儿开始做作业吗？

Friend 1: Schedule A		Friend 2: Schedule B	
9:30 a.m.	打乒乓球	9:30 a.m.	打乒乓球
12:00 p.m.	吃饭	12:30 p.m.	吃饭
2:00 p.m.	买衣服	2:15 p.m.	弹吉他
4:00 p.m.	看篮球比赛	4:00 p.m.	开始做作业
7:00 p.m.	看电影	6:30 p.m.	去饭馆吃饭

Expressing slight discomfort

2a Language Model — TARGET LANGUAGE INPUT

Your teacher will lead a discussion about the images below. Try to participate as much as you can. If there is anything you don't understand, let your teacher know.

Wǒ   yǒu   diǎnr   lěng,   nǐ   lěng   bù   lěng?

我 － 有 － 点儿 － 冷， － 你 － 冷 － 不 － 冷?

I'm kind of cold. Are you cold?

1

lěng

冷

cold

2

rè

热

hot

3

è

饿

hungry

4

kě

渴

thirsty

Chapter 6 • Taking Care of Yourself • Section 2

119

Audio

2b New Words in Context `INTERPRETIVE`

Listen to the audio and try to understand as much as you can. Then read the passage, using the pinyin text and vocabulary list to figure out unfamiliar words.

今天早上不冷也不热，很舒服，所以我跟春月去打网球了。现在是中午，我们都有点儿渴。春月还有点儿累，她想去休息。我不累，可是我有点儿饿。我想去我最喜欢的饭馆吃饭。

Jīntiān zǎoshàng bù **lěng** yě bú **rè**, hěn **shūfu**, suǒyǐ wǒ gēn Chūnyuè
qù dǎ wǎngqiú le. Xiànzài shì zhōngwǔ, wǒmen dōu yǒu diǎnr **kě**.
Chūnyuè hái yǒu diǎnr lèi, tā xiǎng qù **xiūxi**. Wǒ bú lèi, kěshì
wǒ yǒu diǎnr **è**. Wǒ xiǎng qù wǒ zuì xǐhuan de fànguǎn chī fàn.

Comprehension Check

		T	F
1	According to Maya, it was a bit cold this morning.	◯	◯
2	After playing tennis, Isabella and Maya both feel kind of thirsty.	◯	◯
3	Maya and Isabella want to go to Isabella's favorite restaurant to eat.	◯	◯

Vocabulary

Audio

	Word	Pinyin	Meaning
8	冷	lěng	cold
9	热	rè	hot
10	舒服	shūfu	comfortable
11	渴	kě	thirsty
12	休息	xiūxi	to rest, to take a break
13	饿	è	hungry

What a Character!

shuǐ ⟨氵⟩ — 1 氵 2 氵 3 氵

The component 氵 (shuǐ) is commonly referred to as 三点水. Many characters with this component have to do with water or liquid. This component is generally found on the left side of a character.

Look at the words and phrases below. Based on the words you know, try to guess the meaning of each.

xǐ
洗衣服

tāng
喝汤

lèi
泪水

2c Puzzle It Out PROGRESS CHECK

Complete the exercise below to check your understanding of what you learned in Section 2. If you have questions, consult the Language Reference section.

Use the words in the list on the left to complete the translation of each sentence. You may use some words more than once.

一点儿
有点儿
的

1 我 ____ 渴，我想喝 ____ 水。
I am a bit thirsty; I want to drink some water.

2 这本书 ____ 难。
This book is a bit difficult.

3 这个饭馆有你想吃 ____ 菜。
This restaurant has the dish that you want to eat.

3 Using 有(一)点儿 to express "a bit, kind of"

The expression 有（一）点儿 is used before a descriptive word to say that something is a little bit/somewhat [descriptive word]. 有（一）点儿 can also be used before some verbs related to thinking and feeling, such as 想, to say that someone kind of feels a certain way.

1 十点睡觉有（一）点儿晚。 Going to bed at 10 is a bit late.

xiūxi
你今天早点儿休息吧？ Can you go to bed a bit earlier tonight?

2 我有（一）点儿不想去。
I kind of don't want to go. (I don't really want to go.)

shūfu
3 昨天我有（一）点儿不舒服，所以我请假了。
Yesterday I felt a bit unwell, so I asked for a day off (from school).

> **! TAKE NOTE**
>
> 不舒服 (shūfu) is used in many of the same ways "uncomfortable" is used in English, but it can also be used in a different way: to describe feeling sick or under the weather.

4 Using 的 to link something to a phrase that describes it

As discussed previously, 的 can serve as a link between a descriptive word and something being described. 的 can also link a longer descriptive phrase to something being described, similar to "that" in English. Notice that the descriptive phrase always comes before 的, and the thing described always comes after 的.

	descriptive phrase	的	thing described		Meaning
1 这是	我最喜欢看	的	书。		This is my favorite book. (This is the book that I most like to read.)
2	我妈妈送我	的	衣服	很好看！	The clothing that my mom gave me is very nice-looking!
3	喜欢听音乐	的	人	经常去那儿。	People who like to listen to music often go there.

2d Using the Language INTERPERSONAL

Activity 1 Do you find warm weather months or cold weather months more comfortable? In pairs, go through each of the twelve months and discuss whether you find that month hot, a bit hot, comfortable, a bit cold, or cold. Be prepared to share your partner's opinions with the rest of the class. Are there months that everyone agrees on?

Example: 我觉得一月有点儿冷。你觉得呢?

Activity 2 What types of books do you and your classmates like? Get into groups and conduct an interview circle. The teacher will select one student in each group to start the interview. Student 1 will ask the student to the right (student 2) what his/her top three favorite books are. Student 2 will interview the next student to his/her right. Continue in a circle until everyone in the group has been interviewed. Keep track of the answers and be prepared to report back to your teacher. Is there a book that was the favorite of many students? Or does everyone in your class seem to like different books?

我最喜欢看的三本书是⋯⋯

Getting sick

3a Language Model | TARGET LANGUAGE INPUT

Your teacher will lead a discussion about the image below. Try to participate as much as you can. If there is anything you don't understand, let your teacher know.

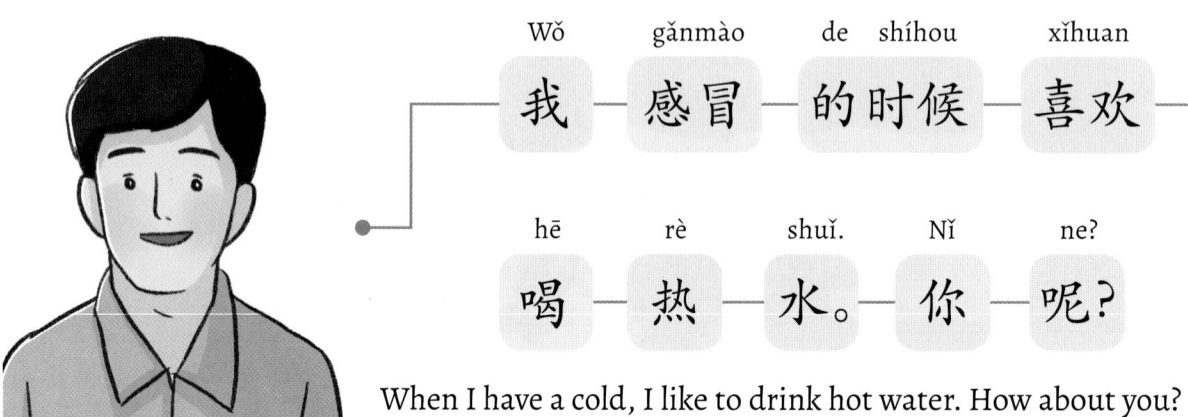

Wǒ	gǎnmào	de shíhou	xǐhuan
我	感冒	的时候	喜欢

hē	rè	shuǐ.	Nǐ	ne?
喝	热	水。	你	呢?

When I have a cold, I like to drink hot water. How about you?

3b New Words in Conversation `INTERPRETIVE`

Listen to the audio and try to understand as much as you can. Then read the dialogue, using the pinyin text and vocabulary list to figure out unfamiliar words.

 Owen 生病 了！我给他
打电话的时候，他跟我
说他感冒了。他头疼，
还有点儿发烧。

Owen **shēng bìng** le! Wǒ gěi tā
dǎ diànhuà de shíhou, tā gēn wǒ
shuō tā **gǎnmào** le. Tā **tóu téng**,
hái yǒu diǎnr **fā shāo**.

 那他什么时候能来学校？

Nà tā shénme shíhou néng **lái** xuéxiào?

 他今天和明天在家休息。
他星期四才能来学校。

Tā jīntiān hé míngtiān zài jiā xiūxi.
Tā xīngqīsì cái néng **lái** xuéxiào.

Comprehension Check

		T	F
1	Owen was running a fever when Miko called him.	○	○
2	Owen will come back to school tomorrow.	○	○

Vocabulary

Audio

	Word	Pinyin	Meaning
14	生病	shēng bìng	to get sick
15	感冒	gǎnmào	common cold; to have a cold, to catch a cold
16	头	tóu	head
17	疼	téng	-ache, aching
18	发烧	fā shāo	to have a fever
19	来	lái	to come

3c Puzzle It Out PROGRESS CHECK

Complete the exercise below to check your understanding of what you learned in Section 3. If you have questions, consult the Language Reference section.

Rearrange the Chinese words and phrases in each row to translate the English sentences.

1 我头 ︳ 不想 ︳ 看 ︳ 疼 ︳ 的时候 ︳ 电视。

   When I have a headache, I don't want to watch TV.

2 的时候 ︳ 听 ︳ 我做作业 ︳ 音乐。 ︳ 喜欢

   When I do my homework, I like listening to music.

3 中文课 ︳ 你上 ︳ 的时候 ︳ 说 ︳ 能不能 ︳ 英文?

   Can you speak English when you're in Chinese class?

Language Reference •

5 Describing a specific time or situation with 的时候

A time phrase is created when 的时候 follows a specific time or situation. The time phrase is often translated as a "when" phrase and usually comes at the beginning of the sentence. When the subject of the sentence (highlighted below in gray) is stated in the time phrase, it is not repeated later in the sentence.

1 我发烧的时候不想去学校上课。
   fāshāo

   When I have a fever, I don't want to go to school.

2 他做饭的时候喜欢听音乐。

   He likes listening to music while he is cooking.

3 我紧张的时候很想喝水。

   When I'm nervous, I really want to drink water.

4 我在中国的时候，爸爸经常给我打电话。

   When I was in China, my father called me frequently.

How does being sick affect what you want to do? Think of activities that are a part of your normal routine but that you can't or don't like to do when you are sick. Also, think of things that you *only* do when you are sick. Discuss with a partner. Be prepared to tell the class about your habits when you are sick and listen to your classmates' responses. What were the two most common things mentioned that students do/do not want to do when they are sick?

Example:

我经常做运动。可是生病的时候，我不想做运动。

You know that 头 (tóu) + 疼 (téng) means "headache." Look up the Chinese words for these other conditions.

toothache

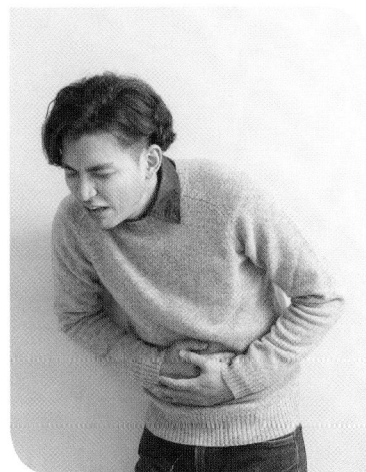
stomachache

sore throat
(literally "throat ache")

Put the Pieces Together!

Audio

A Reading and Listening INTERPRETIVE

Passage 1

EMMA AND ISABELLA ARE EATING BREAKFAST AND GETTING READY TO GO, BUT MARTIN DOESN'T SEEM TO BE UP YET.

① 春月，
马丁起床了吗？

不知道……
马丁！马丁！……

② 妈妈、春月，
我起床了……

③ 好，吃吧。
今天早点儿去学校。

可是我现在不太饿……

④ 你很冷吗，
马丁？

我觉得很冷，还有点儿头疼……
Ah choo! Ah choo! Ah choo!

⑤ 你是不是感冒了？

129

Comprehension Check

		T	F
1	Martin feels cold and hungry.	○	○
2	Isabella asks if Martin has a cold.	○	○
3	According to Emma, Martin has a bit of a fever.	○	○
4	Martin asks Emma for some hot water to drink.	○	○
5	Emma will call the school to report Martin as absent.	○	○

Passage 2 Look at this thermometer, which gives temperature in degrees Celsius. What temperatures are labeled as "cold" and what temperatures are labeled as "hot"? Do you see any other words you recognize on this thermometer?

Passage 3 Listen to Ellen and Martin's conversation about Isabella. Answer the questions on a separate piece of paper.

1 What makes Ellen think that Isabella might be sick?
  (a) Isabella called her and told her.
  (b) Isabella didn't come to school at her usual time.
  (c) Isabella told her she couldn't play ping-pong this afternoon.

2 What symptoms does Isabella have?
  (a) She has a fever.
  (b) She feels hot all the time.
  (c) She doesn't want to eat or drink anything.

3 What does Ellen say Isabella needs to do to get better soon?
  (a) Stay at home and rest.
  (b) Go to sleep earlier.
  (c) Drink a lot of cold water.

Passage 4 Listen to the phone conversation. Then, on a separate piece of paper, write the letter of each event in the order that the girl will do them.

B Speaking INTERPERSONAL

Imagine that you're preparing to visit a school in China. Before you go, you want to know what some of their class rules are. With a partner, brainstorm a list of questions you have about class rules in China. When one of you thinks of a question, both of you should guess whether that activity is allowed in class in China. The Word Bank shows possible activities for you to discuss, but feel free to search for other words that express the activities you personally want to ask about.

上课的时候，我们能不能……?
我们能不能晚点儿……?

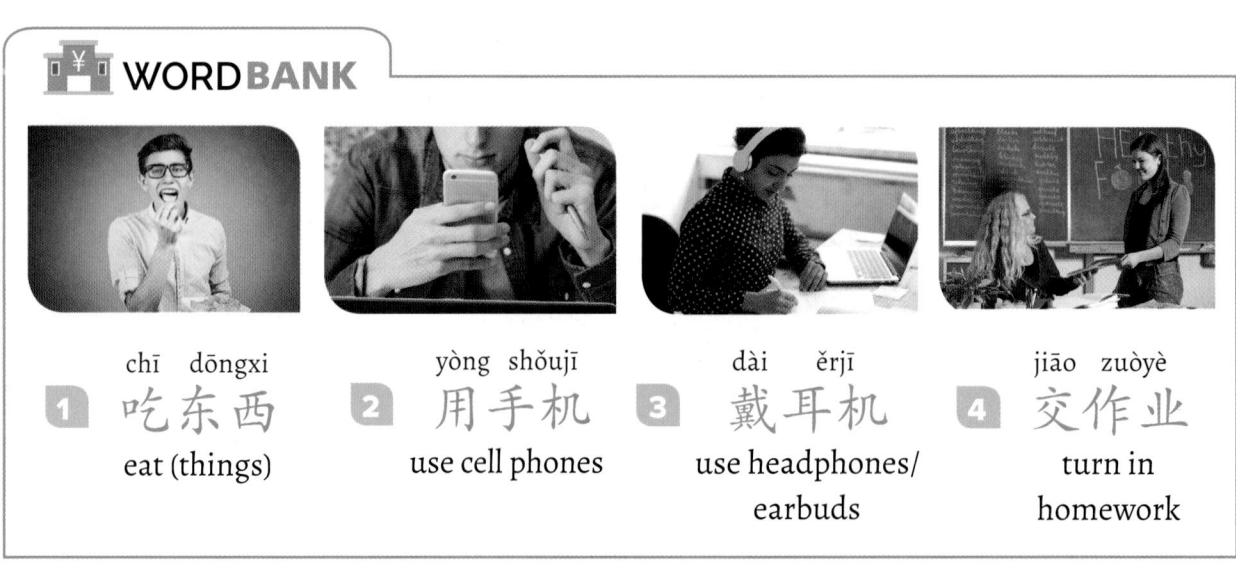

WORD BANK

chī dōngxi	yòng shǒujī	dài ěrjī	jiāo zuòyè
1 吃东西	**2** 用手机	**3** 戴耳机	**4** 交作业
eat (things)	use cell phones	use headphones/earbuds	turn in homework

C   Final Project   PRESENTATIONAL

Public Service Announcement

Step 1: In pairs, discuss what advice you would give to someone who is sick. Pick one piece of advice that you think should be communicated to the public. You will create a poster to illustrate this advice as a public service announcement.

Step 2: Because this poster is a public service announcement, you will need to be very direct and tell people what they must do and are not allowed to do. (Hint: Use 可以, 得, or 不能.) Be sure to include both text and visuals to make your message informative and interesting.

生病的时候……

Can-Do Goals

Talk with your teacher if you have questions or if you are not certain you can do the following tasks:

- Understand things Chinese students might do to stay healthy
- Talk about what you can do and what the situation allows you to do
- Discuss adjusting plans to do something a bit earlier or later
- Understand when others say they are hungry, thirsty, hot, or cold
- Talk about common health problems
- Express what you do (and do not do) when you are sick

Cultural Knowledge

If you're not feeling well, what might a Chinese friend tell you to do?

A BALANCED SCHEDULE

In Unit 3, you will learn to talk about study habits and extracurricular clubs. You will also learn to describe a sequence of events and to say what might happen in the future.

The student band at No. 7 High School in Chengdu performs in a concert

Essential Question
How do you decide what to spend time on outside of class?

CHAPTER 7
Looking for Support

Martin is having difficulty managing his time and asks Isabella about her strategies.

CHAPTER 8
Making Progress

Maya helps Martin during an after-school study session.

CHAPTER 9
School and Activities

At a Chinese Club gathering, Martin and his friends reflect on the past semester.

At the end of the unit, you will play the role of an advice columnist for the student newspaper. You will:

- Read brief letters from students describing problems that they are facing

- Talk with a partner about those problems and brainstorm suggestions you could offer

- Write an advice column to respond to the students' letters

Looking for Support

Isabella: Mom, where's Martin? I'm about to leave for school.

Emma: I think he just woke up. He went to bed pretty late last night, so he overslept again today.

Isabella: Why is he always up so late?! I can't wait for him; I'm going to head out now.

Emma: Okay, I'll let him know. Have a good day at school!

Can-Do Goals

In this chapter, you will learn to:

- Understand ways Chinese students might look for academic support
- Discuss doing something again
- Understand when someone describes a sequence of events
- Talk about completing a task
- Advise someone to do more or less of something
- Express things that will happen or that could happen

xuéxí   fǔzhù

学习辅助

Academic Support

It's common for Chinese students to look for support beyond the classroom, either to boost their grades or to get help preparing for exams. Also, some rural school districts may seek outside resources to supplement their limited academic offerings.

Supplemental Books

In addition to their school-issued textbooks, many students in China use supplemental reference books and workbooks to reinforce their learning. Bookstores offer a variety of learning materials to choose from. Here, customers browse a bookstore in Jiangmen, Guangdong Province.

Tutoring

Stiff competition to get into good colleges has made private tutoring common for middle and high school students in China. Tutors are often college or graduate school students.

Going Digital

Digital education is a growing trend in China, with many providers offering specialized supplemental learning for middle and high school students, such as online English tutoring from native speakers. In rural areas, where both teachers and classroom resources can be limited, the Chinese government has tried to improve education quality by giving thousands of students access to a range of online courses.

By the Numbers

Since 2012, the amount of money earned by companies in the online education market in China has grown by 20 to 30 percent each year.

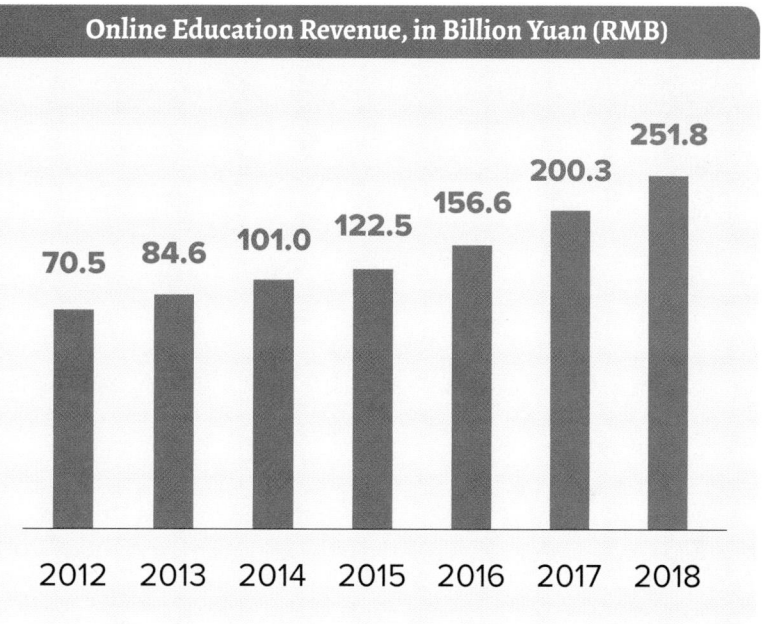

Online Education Revenue, in Billion Yuan (RMB)

2012	2013	2014	2015	2016	2017	2018
70.5	84.6	101.0	122.5	156.6	200.3	251.8

Source: iResearch Consulting Group, 2019

REFLECT ON THE ESSENTIAL QUESTION

How do you decide what to spend time on outside of class?

1. What learning supports are available to you and your friends beyond the classroom? How do they compare with the kinds of support described here?

2. Have you ever asked for extra help before a test?

3. Can you recall a time when someone tutored you, or you tutored someone else, in a difficult subject?

Again?

1a Language Model TARGET LANGUAGE INPUT

Your teacher will lead a discussion about the image below. Try to participate as much as you can. If there is anything you don't understand, let your teacher know.

Nǐ	zuótiān	yòu	qù	wèn	lǎoshī	wèntí	le	ma?
你	昨天	又	去	问	老师	问题	了	吗?

Did you go ask the teacher questions again yesterday?

Nǐ	míngtiān	hái	yào	zài	qù	wèn	lǎoshī	wèntí	ma?
你	明天	还	要	再	去	问	老师	问题	吗?

Are you going to go ask the teacher questions again tomorrow?

1	2
yòu	zài
又	再
again	again

Audio

Listen to the audio and try to understand as much as you can. Then read the passage, using the pinyin text and vocabulary list to figure out unfamiliar words.

今天我又去问老师问题了。明天我还想再去问老师问题。明天我想先问数学老师一个问题，再问中文老师两个问题，然后问历史老师一个问题，最后问科学老师三个问题。

Jīntiān wǒ yòu qù wèn lǎoshī wèntí le. Míngtiān wǒ hái xiǎng zài qù wèn lǎoshī wèntí. Míngtiān wǒ xiǎng xiān wèn shùxué lǎoshī yí gè wèntí, zài wèn Zhōngwén lǎoshī liǎng gè wèntí, ránhòu wèn lìshǐ lǎoshī yí gè wèntí, zuìhòu wèn kēxué lǎoshī sān gè wèntí.

Comprehension Check

		T	F
1	According to the passage, Ellen asked her teachers some questions yesterday.	○	○
2	Ellen wants to ask her science teacher a question first, then ask her Chinese teacher some questions.	○	○

Vocabulary

Audio

	Word	Pinyin	Meaning
1	又	yòu	again
2	问题	wèntí	problem, question
3	还	hái	still, yet; also
4	再	zài	again; then
5	先	xiān	first
6	然后	ránhòu	and then
7	最后	zuìhòu	final, last; finally, lastly

1c Puzzle It Out PROGRESS CHECK

Complete the exercise below to check your understanding of what you learned in Section 1. If you have questions, consult the Language Reference section.

Rearrange these sentences to create a story. Pay close attention to the words that indicate the sequence of events.

1 昨天中午我们去饭馆吃饭了。我先点了一份面条。

2 最后我还给我爸爸点了一份饺子。

3 今天中午我们又去饭馆吃了饺子、面条和红烧肉。

4 然后我点了一份红烧肉。

5 可是我说："今天晚上我们再去饭馆吃饭吧？"

6 现在是晚上七点，我们还没吃饭。爸爸说他要去做饭了。

Language Reference

1 Saying that something is still the case

In addition to meaning "also," 还 can mean "still" or "yet."

1 她还没有开始做作业。

She still hasn't started doing her homework. / She hasn't started doing her homework yet.

2 今天中午我吃了十六个饺子，可是现在还觉得有点儿饿。

Today at lunch I ate sixteen dumplings, but I still feel a bit hungry right now.

2 Uses of 又 and 再

又 (yòu) and 再 (zài) can both mean "again." They come just before the main action word or phrase in a sentence. 又 (yòu) is typically used when talking about events or actions that were repeated in the past, and 再 (zài) is mostly used to talk about the possibility of a repeated event or action in the future.

1 我哥哥^{yòu}又给我打电话了。

My older brother called me again.

Go Far with Chinese

2 我昨天没有去打乒乓球，我今天<ruby>又<rt>yòu</rt></ruby>没有去打乒乓球。

I didn't play ping-pong yesterday, and I didn't play ping-pong today either.

3 我明天<ruby>再<rt>zài</rt></ruby>给你打电话。

I'll call you again tomorrow.

再 (zài) can also mean "then." So 先 (xiān)...再 (zài) and 先 (xiān)...然后 (ránhòu) mean "first...then." 先 (xiān)...再 (zài) is used to describe the sequence of activities that are a part of a routine or that happen regularly. Also, 先 (xiān)...再 (zài) can give the order of events that will happen in the future, while 先 (xiān)...然后 (ránhòu) can be used when referring to both past and future events.

4 他早上喜欢<ruby>先<rt>xiān</rt></ruby>喝点儿热水，<ruby>再<rt>zài</rt></ruby>吃饭。

In the morning, he likes to drink some hot water first, then have breakfast.

5 我想<ruby>先<rt>xiān</rt></ruby>去给她买礼物，<ruby>再<rt>zài</rt></ruby>去看电影。

I want to go buy a gift for her first, then go see a movie.

6 我昨天<ruby>先<rt>xiān</rt></ruby>去给她买了礼物，<ruby>然后<rt>ránhòu</rt></ruby>去看了一个电影。

Yesterday, I went to buy a gift for her first, then I went to see a movie.

LANGUAGE CHALLENGE

Here is a Chinese expression that means you are running out of chances:

有<ruby>再<rt>zài</rt></ruby>一<ruby>再<rt>zài</rt></ruby>二，没有<ruby>再<rt>zài</rt></ruby>三<ruby>再<rt>zài</rt></ruby>四。

Can you write a rough translation of this saying?

The chart below shows routine activities for four students. Your teacher will assign you the identity of one of the students.

Step 1: Imagine that it is Wednesday evening. Using the chart, write at least three sentences that describe your activities for the week.

- Write one sentence about something you did earlier this week and then did again on Wednesday.
- Write one sentence about something you did on Wednesday and you plan to do again later in the week.
- Write one sentence describing the order in which you did activities on one day.

Step 2: Read the sentences you wrote to a partner. Based on this information, your partner will try to guess your identity. If he or she can't guess who you are from your description, your partner will ask follow up questions. Then switch and try to guess your partner's identity.

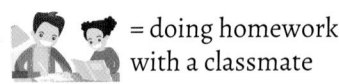 = doing homework with a classmate   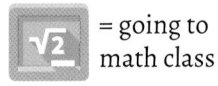 = going to math class   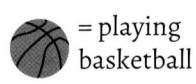 = playing basketball   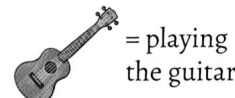 = playing the guitar

	星期一	星期二 先	星期二 然后	星期三 先	星期三 然后	星期四 先	星期四 然后	星期五 先	星期五 然后
小明	homework	math	homework	math	guitar	math	basketball	guitar	basketball
欢欢	homework	homework	basketball	guitar	basketball	basketball	homework	math	guitar
小天	homework	guitar	math	homework	guitar	math	guitar	basketball	homework
乐乐	homework	basketball	guitar	homework	basketball	homework	math	guitar	math

Study plans

2a Language Model — TARGET LANGUAGE INPUT

Your teacher will lead a discussion about the images below. Try to participate as much as you can. If there is anything you don't understand, let your teacher know.

Tā de jìhuà shì duō fùxí, shǎo kàn
她 的 计划 是 多 复习, 少 看

diànshì. Nǐ yě yǒu xuéxí jìhuà ma?
电视。 你 也 有 学习 计划 吗?

Her plan is to review (study) more and watch TV less. Do you also have study plans?

1

yùxí

预习

to preview, to study
(materials not yet taught in class)

2

fùxí

复习

to review, to study
(materials already taught)

2b New Words in Context `INTERPRETIVE`

Listen to the audio and try to understand as much as you can. Then read the passage, using the pinyin text and vocabulary list to figure out unfamiliar words.

我朋友告诉我，她今天做了一个学习计划。她计划晚上七点十分做完作业，然后多做预习和复习，少看电视。我觉得她的计划挺好的！

Wǒ péngyou **gàosu** wǒ, tā jīntiān zuò le yí gè **xuéxí jìhuà**. Tā **jìhuà** wǎnshàng qī diǎn shí fēn zuò **wán** zuòyè, ránhòu duō zuò **yùxí** hé **fùxí**, **shǎo** kàn diànshì. Wǒ juéde tā de **jìhuà** tǐng hǎo de!

Comprehension Check

		T	F
1	Miko's friend plans to finish her homework before reviewing and previewing her classwork.	○	○
2	According to Miko, her friend plans to watch TV more.	○	○

Vocabulary

Audio

	Word	Pinyin	Meaning
8	告诉	gàosu	to tell
9	学习	xuéxí	studies; to study, to learn
10	计划	jìhuà	plan; to plan
11	完	wán	to finish, to complete
12	预习	yùxí	to preview, to study (materials not yet taught in class)
13	复习	fùxí	to review, to study (materials already taught)
14	少	shǎo	few, not many, less

2c Puzzle It Out

Complete the exercise below to check your understanding of what you learned in Section 2. If you have questions, consult the Language Reference section.

Rearrange the Chinese words and phrases in each row to translate the English sentences.

1 书 | 完 | 他们 | 买 | 了。
They finished buying books.

2 多 | 菜 | 做 | 吧。 | 点儿
Make a few more dishes.

3 她 | 英文， | 多 | 少 | 说 | 想 | 中文。 | 说
She wants to speak less English and more Chinese.

Language Reference

3 Completing or finishing something

完 (wán) comes directly after the main action word in a sentence and indicates whether or not the action has been completed. To say that something is not yet finished, use 没有 rather than 不 (see example 3).

	main action word	wán 完		Meaning
1	她	看	完	电影了。	She finished watching the movie.
2	老师	说	完	了。	The teacher has finished speaking.
3	他还没有	做	完	饭。	He still hasn't finished cooking.
4	你	做	完	作业了吗?	Have you finished your homework?

4 Doing something more or less

多 and 少 (shǎo) can be used immediately before a main action word. When used this way, they mean roughly "to do more of" something and "to do less of" something.

1 感冒的时候得多喝水。
When you have a cold, you need to drink more water.

2 你得少看电影，多复习。
shǎo · · · fùxí
You should watch movies less, and study more.

3 多在家做饭，少去饭馆吃饭。
· · · · shǎo
Cook at home more; eat out at restaurants less.

2d Using the Language INTERPERSONAL / PRESENTATIONAL

Activity 1 Chinese parents often tell their kids 多喝点儿热水. What advice do you often receive from your parents, teachers, and friends? Survey your classmates about the advice in the chart below. What advice do your classmates often get?

Example: 有没有人经常跟你说："你得多看书"?

WORD BANK

1 多看书

2 少看电视

3 多喝水

4 多做运动

5 多吃菜

6 少买衣服

Activity 2 Yesterday evening 李然 forgot that he had band practice and rushed out in the middle of dinner. Draw a picture of his home just after he left showing that he finished some activities but was right in the middle of doing others. Show your picture to a classmate — can your partner describe what 李然 had and had not yet finished?

What a Character!

This component comes from the character 手 (shǒu), meaning "hand." Characters with this component may relate to actions done with the hands.

This image shows someone's afternoon/evening schedule. Can you find the characters containing 扌 (shǒu)? What do you notice about the location of the 扌 (shǒu) component? Ask your teacher about any words you do not recognize. (A few of the unfamiliar words shown here can be found on the next page.)

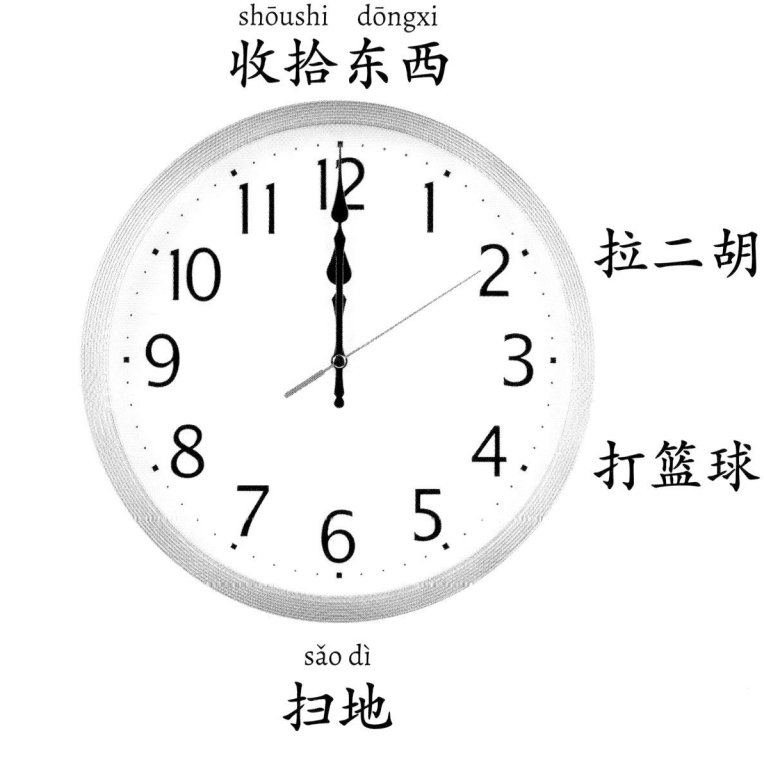

Expressing what will happen

3a Language Model   TARGET LANGUAGE INPUT

Your teacher will lead a discussion about the images below. Try to participate as much as you can. If there is anything you don't understand, let your teacher know.

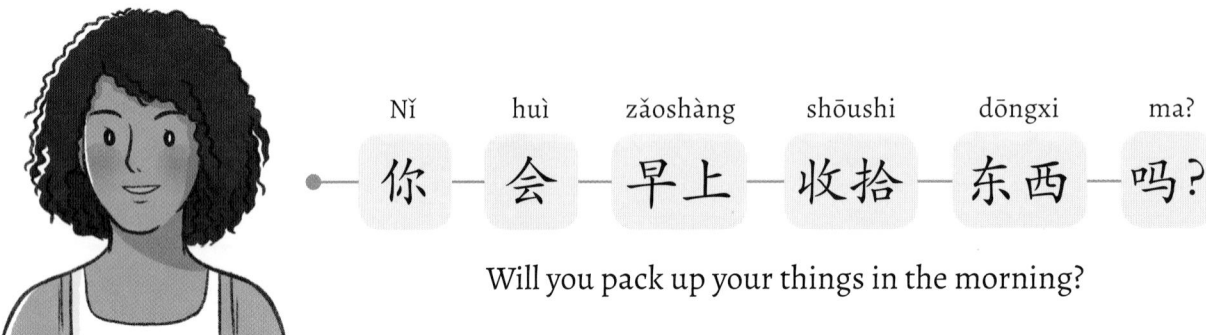

Nǐ	huì	zǎoshàng	shōushi	dōngxi	ma?
你	会	早上	收拾	东西	吗?

Will you pack up your things in the morning?

1

shōushi dōngxi

收拾东西

to pack things up, to tidy up, to put things away

Audio

Isabella and Martin are getting ready for school. Listen to their conversation and try to understand as much as you can. Then read the dialogue, using the pinyin text and vocabulary list to figure out unfamiliar words.

马丁，别吃了……如果
你还不开始收拾东西，
你今天一定会迟到！

Mǎdīng, bié chī le...Rúguǒ
nǐ hái bù kāishǐ shōushi dōngxi,
nǐ jīntiān yídìng huì chídào!

我知道了，春月！

Wǒ zhīdào le, Chūnyuè!

你要我帮你收拾东西吗？

Nǐ yào wǒ bāng nǐ shōushi dōngxi ma?

不用，不用……

Búyòng, búyòng...

Comprehension Check

		T	F
1	Isabella asks Martin to stop eating and finish his homework.	◯	◯
2	Isabella is concerned that Martin will be late.	◯	◯

Vocabulary

Audio

	Word	Pinyin	Meaning
15	别	bié	don't (in advice or a command)
16	如果	rúguǒ	if
17	收拾	shōushi	to pack (up), to tidy (up), to put things away
18	东西	dōngxi	thing(s)
19	会	huì	will; can, know how to
20	迟到	chídào	to be late, to arrive late
21	帮	bāng	to help

5Cs

COMPARISONS

COMMUNITIES
COMMUNICATION
CULTURES
CONNECTIONS

When using a simple word or phrase to respond to someone in Chinese, it is common to say it multiple times, sometimes to soften the tone and other times to emphasize a reaction. For example, if someone asked 这是你要的书吗？, you could respond with 对，对，对 . Or you might say 不用，不用 when turning down someone's offer of help.

Do you ever repeat your response? In what situations?

3c Puzzle It Out PROGRESS CHECK

Complete the exercise below to check your understanding of what you learned in Section 3. If you have questions, consult the Language Reference section.

Read the Chinese, then choose the best English translation.

1 我饿了，我们去吃饭吧。
(a) I was hungry, so we ate rice.
(b) I'm hungry — let's go eat.

2 你同学后天会不会来我们家？
(a) Is your classmate coming over to our house the day after tomorrow?
(b) Does your classmate know how to come to our house the day after tomorrow?

3 今天晚上我会在家做饭。
(a) I will make dinner at home tonight.
(b) I learned how to cook tonight.

4 已经九点半了，可是我还没做完作业。
(a) It's already 9:30, but I still haven't finished my homework.
(b) At 9:30, I still hadn't done my homework.

5 **Expressing a change in situation with 了**

In addition to expressing a completed action, the word 了 can be used to indicate that a change has occurred in a situation or in someone's condition.

1 我饿了。   I'm hungry! (I wasn't before, but I am now!)

bié
2 别吃了。   Stop eating. (You were eating before, but now you should not.)

3 已经八点半了！   It's already 8:30! (It wasn't 8:30 before, but now it is.)

4 我会打乒乓球了。   I (now) know how to play ping-pong.

6 **Talking about possible events**

会 expresses that a future action or event will probably happen. When used this way, 会 is similar to the English "will."

1 他明天会不会去看足球比赛？
   Will he go watch the soccer game tomorrow?

2 我下个星期不会去看她。
   I won't go to see her next week.

3 姐，大明说他星期六会给你打电话。
   Sis, Daming said that he'll call you on Saturday.

Sometimes 会 is used when talking about things that could happen or could have happened if the situation were different, carrying a meaning similar to "would."

rúguǒ   chídào
4 如果你不早点儿起床，你每天都会迟到！
   If you don't get up a bit earlier, you will be late every day!

rúguǒ
5 如果你可以买一只宠物，你会选狗还是猫？
   If you were allowed to buy a pet, would you choose a dog or a cat?

Activity 1 As a class, brainstorm sentences that introduce a change of situation using 了. Then play Charades! Students will take turns randomly selecting one of the brainstormed sentences and acting out the scenario without making any sounds. When you think you know what your classmate is acting out, raise your hand. If your teacher calls on you, say the sentence you think your classmate is acting out.

Activity 2 Who would you turn to for help in your studies? In pairs, ask each other about who you would ask for help if you had difficulty with the homework for different classes (science, English, Chinese, math, history) — a parent, sibling, teacher, or classmate? Why would you go to those people for help? Do you and your partner have the same people in mind, or would you go to different people?

Example:

如果你做历史作业的时候有问题，你会问谁？为什么？

Put the Pieces Together!

A Reading and Listening INTERPRETIVE

Audio

Passage 1

THE LOPEZES HAVE ALL RECENTLY ARRIVED HOME AND ARE ABOUT TO HAVE DINNER.

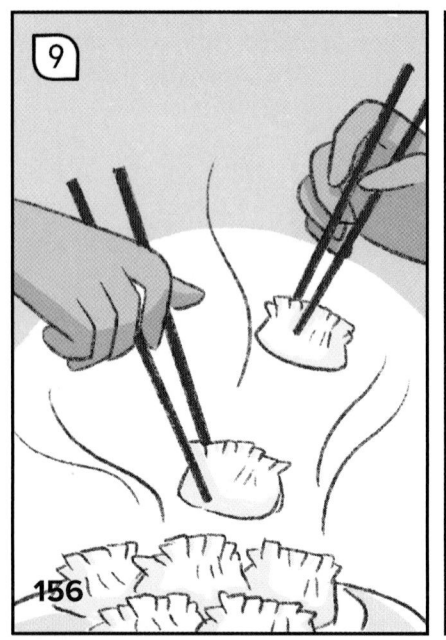

Comprehension Check ✓

1. Martin was late to school for the first time today. ○ T ○ F
2. Martin went to bed right after he finished his math homework. ○ T ○ F
3. Isabella does homework as well as preview and review work every day. ○ T ○ F
4. Because she has so much to do every day, Isabella is also late to school sometimes. ○ T ○ F

Passage 2 Read the saying on this pencil case. Can you guess what the advice is based on the first four characters?

Passage 3 Listen to the conversation between Sanjay, Leo, and Maya and then answer the questions below.

		T	F
1	Sanjay thinks that if you preview the classwork, you will find the class more interesting.	○	○
2	Maya thinks that if you review every day, you'll find that homework is easy to do.	○	○
3	Leo thinks that previewing is more important than reviewing.	○	○

B Speaking INTERPERSONAL

How much do you know about your classmates' lives? In pairs, ask about each other's weekend plans. See the Word Bank on the opposite page for additional activities you might want to talk about. When you describe your plans for Saturday and Sunday, mention three to four activities for each day — but make at least one of those activities false (and at least one true)! Then your partner will guess which activities you will not be doing.

Q: 你这个周末的计划是什么？ / 你这个周末有什么计划？

A: 我这个周末的计划是：星期六我想先……再…… 然后……最后……

fángjiān

1 收拾房间

tidy one's room

wánr

2 跟朋友一起玩儿

hang out with friends

xiǎoshuō

3 看小说

read a novel

gōng

4 打工

work (at a part-time job)

yìgōng

5 做义工

do volunteer work

biānchéng

6 学编程

learn coding

C Final Project PRESENTATIONAL

Giving Advice

Read about the problems this student is encountering. With your partner, discuss how to help him/her, then write a response to him/her with your advice.

我每天都会先看电视，然后弹吉他，最后做作业。我觉得每门课的作业都很难，所以有的时候我十一点才能做完作业。有的时候我还会迟到。

Talk with your teacher if you have questions or if you are not certain you can do the following tasks:

- Understand ways Chinese students might look for academic support
- Discuss doing something again
- Understand when someone describes a sequence of events
- Talk about completing a task
- Advise someone to do more or less of something
- Express things that will happen or that could happen

Cultural Knowledge

In what ways do Chinese students try to improve their knowledge outside the classroom?

Making Progress

Martin: Hey Maya, are you free after school today?

Maya: I think so. Why?

Martin: I was wondering if we could do homework together. When I do homework by myself, sometimes I start too late. . .

Maya: Sure! Could we meet at 4:00?

Martin: Sounds good. See you then!

Can-Do Goals

In this chapter, you will learn to:

- Explore fun activities to support Chinese learning outside the classroom
- Describe your impression of different activities
- Say that you or others were mistaken in their thinking
- Discuss what you have done before
- Understand when someone emphasizes what something is or who someone is
- Describe how a situation changes over time

yìshù   hé   Zhōngwén   xuéxí

艺术和中文学习
The Arts and Chinese Learning

For fun and to support their learning, students of Chinese often explore Chinese arts and entertainment. Here are a few activities popular among Chinese language learners.

Chinese Calligraphy

Besides reinforcing the finer points of writing Chinese characters, learning the thousands-year-old art of Chinese calligraphy can help calm the mind and focus attention, similar to meditation. There might be a Chinese calligraphy class in your community, but if not, there are many online tutorial videos!

C-Pop

Short for "Chinese popular music," C-pop is performed by artists in places where Chinese is widely spoken, including China, Malaysia, and Singapore. Ever thought of forming a group and trying to sing along?

C-pop singer Li Yuchun performs in Shanghai

162

Chinese Dramas

Watching Chinese television series, sometimes called C-dramas, could be the perfect way to get in a little entertainment while learning Chinese! These programs may be funny, romantic, or action-packed. Many historical C-dramas are filmed at Hengdian World Studios in Zhejiang Province, pictured here.

By the Numbers

Every year, TV stations across China broadcast millions of drama episodes.

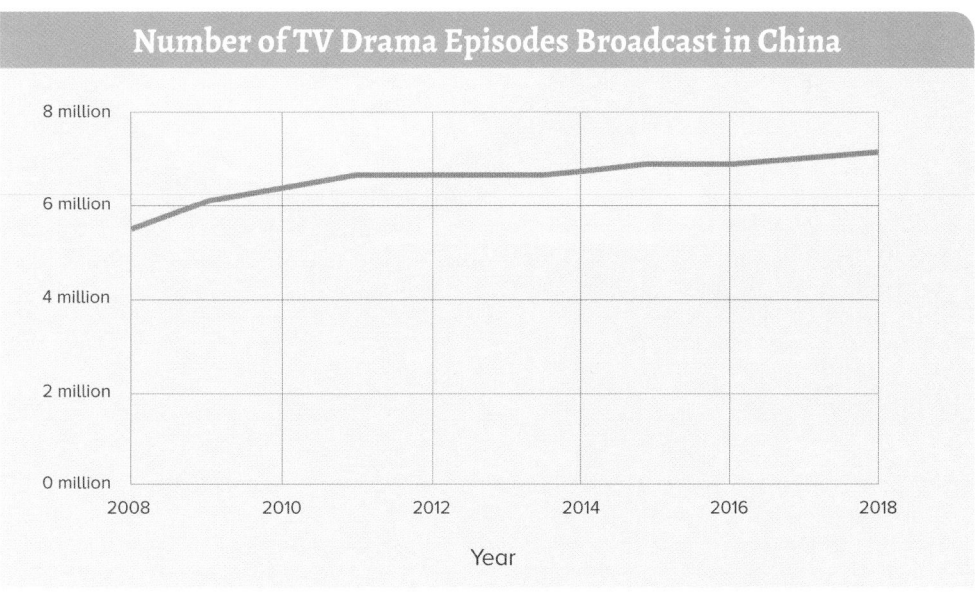

Number of TV Drama Episodes Broadcast in China

Year

Source: National Bureau of Statistics of China, 2018

REFLECT ON THE ESSENTIAL QUESTION

How do you decide what to spend time on outside of class?

1. Do you seek out Chinese arts, music, and shows? Why or why not?

2. What kinds of activities do you think would make learning Chinese more fun for you? What about them appeals to you?

3. Imagine a Chinese student learning English. What kinds of arts or entertainment would you suggest to them as a way to boost their English skills?

Learning Chinese

1a Language Model TARGET LANGUAGE INPUT

Your teacher will lead a discussion about the image below. Try to participate as much as you can. If there is anything you don't understand, let your teacher know.

Nǐ	juéde	Zhōngwén	xué	qǐ	lái	yǒuyìsi	ma?
你	觉得	中文	学	起来	有意思	吗?

Do you think learning Chinese is fun?

Audio

Listen to the audio and try to understand as much as you can. Then read the dialogue, using the pinyin text and vocabulary list to figure out unfamiliar words.

以前我以为中文不太好学，但是现在我觉得中文学起来挺容易的！

Yǐqián wǒ yǐwéi Zhōngwén bú tài hǎo xué, dànshì xiànzài wǒ juéde Zhōngwén xué qǐ lái tǐng róngyì de!

是啊，而且我觉得中文的语法很好懂。

Shì a, érqiě wǒ juéde Zhōngwén de yǔfǎ hěn hǎo dǒng.

Comprehension Check

                                                        T   F

1   Before, Owen assumed that Chinese was not easy to learn.   ○   ○

2   Ellen thinks that Chinese grammar is easy to understand.   ○   ○

Vocabulary

Audio

	Word	Pinyin	Meaning
1	以前	yǐqián	before, ago
2	以为	yǐwéi	to mistakenly think, to assume incorrectly
3	但是	dànshì	but, however
4	起来	qǐ lái	(a word that follows a verb and is used to introduce an impression)
5	容易	róngyì	easy
6	语法	yǔfǎ	grammar
7	懂	dǒng	to understand

Complete the exercise below to check your understanding of what you learned in Section 1. If you have questions, consult the Language Reference section.

Rearrange the Chinese words and phrases in each row to translate the English sentences.

1 吉他 ｜ 很难。｜ 学 ｜ 起来
Learning to play the guitar is difficult.

2 起来 ｜ 听 ｜ 这个 ｜ 很好。｜ 主意
This idea sounds good.

3 不太 ｜ 作业 ｜ 起来 ｜ 看 ｜ 今天的 ｜ 好做。
Today's homework looks hard (to do).

Language Reference ●

1 Indicating an impression or judgement

起来 (qǐ lái) has a number of different meanings, including "to stand up" or "to get up." However, in the following examples, 起来 (qǐ lái) indicates that upon/after doing something, the speaker is left with a certain impression. When used this way, 起来 (qǐ lái) comes after a verb and before a description.

1 网球学^{qǐ lái}起来挺难的！
Learning to play tennis is quite difficult!

2 这门课看^{qǐ lái}起来很有意思。
This course looks/seems very interesting.

3 这个菜看^{qǐ lái}起来好看，吃^{qǐ lái}起来也很好吃。
This dish looks good, and it also tastes good.

4 说^{qǐ lái róngyì}起来容易，做^{qǐ lái}起来难。
Easier said than done. (Saying it is easy, doing it is difficult.)

Come up with three things that you used to think were difficult to do, but you now think are easy. In groups, go around the circle and tell your classmates about them. Keep track of everyone's answers. Are there certain activities that many people thought were difficult but now find easy?

Example:

A: 你以前以为什么学起来很难？现在呢？
B: 我以前以为吉他学起来很难，现在觉得挺容易的。

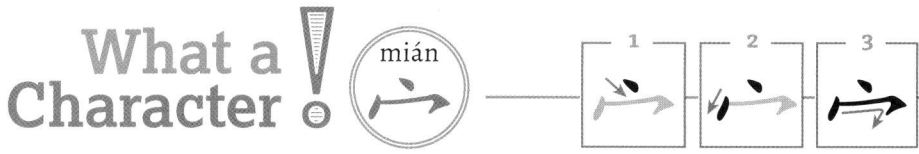

The component 宀 (mián) appears in many characters, including 容易 (róngyì) and 家. Although 宀 (mián) means "roof" or "cover," characters with this component can have a wide variety of meanings.

Which words have the 宀 (mián) component? Look carefully! 宀 (mián) is easy to confuse with 冖 (mì) or 亠 (tóu). A couple of strokes make all the difference!

xiě
写
to write

kètīng
客厅
living room

jiàoshì
教室
classroom

tíngzi
亭子
pavillion

Discussing past experiences

2a Language Model TARGET LANGUAGE INPUT

Your teacher will lead a discussion about the images below. Try to participate as much as you can. If there is anything you don't understand, let your teacher know.

Nǐ	zuò	guò	zhège	tí	ma?
你	做	过	这个	题	吗?

Have you done this problem before?

Dá'àn	jiù	shì	zhège	ma?
答案	就	是	这个	吗?

Is the answer exactly this?

1

tí

题

question, problem
(in homework or on a test)

2

dá'àn

答案

answer

2b New Words in Conversation INTERPRETIVE

Listen to the audio and try to understand as much as you can. Then read the dialogue, using the pinyin text and vocabulary list to figure out unfamiliar words.

 老师说过这个题的答案。
答案就是 A，不是 B。

Lǎoshī shuō guò zhège tí de dá'àn.
Dá'àn jiù shì A, bú shì B.

 那我的答案错了……
你会做这个题吗？
你可以教我做吗？

Nà wǒ de dá'àn cuò le....
Nǐ huì zuò zhège tí ma?
Nǐ kěyǐ jiāo wǒ zuò ma?

 可以啊。

Kěyǐ a.

 太好了，谢谢！

Tài hǎo le, xièxie!

 不客气！

Bú kèqi!

Comprehension Check

		T	F
1	The teacher told the students the correct answer before.	○	○
2	Leo's answer was correct.	○	○

Vocabulary

Audio

	Word	Pinyin	Meaning
8	过	guò	(word used after a verb to indicate a past experience)
9	题	tí	question, problem (in homework or on a test)
10	答案	dá'àn	answer
11	就	jiù	precisely, exactly
12	错	cuò	wrong, incorrect
13	客气	kèqi	polite; to be polite/courteous

LANGUAGE CHALLENGE

Take a look at the photo below. There are many ways to use 客气 (kèqi) in polite exchanges. Try to figure out what each person is saying.

你们太客气了。谢谢!

别客气。

不用客气。

你跟我们客气什么啊!

2c Puzzle It Out PROGRESS CHECK

Complete the exercises below to check your understanding of what you learned in Section 2. If you have questions, consult the Language Reference section.

Exercise 1 Rearrange these sentences to create a story.

1 我弟弟以前没有看过中国电影。

2 他今天跟同学说:"我看过中国电影。中国电影很好看!"

3 昨天他问我:"我们可以去哪儿看中国电影? 你知道吗?"

4 然后,我们昨天晚上一起去看了一个中国电影。

5 我说:"知道啊。我看过很多中国电影。"

Exercise 2 Isabella asked Martin something, and his possible answers are below. Select the answer that shows more certainty and emphasis.

春月："这不是我的书。这是你的书。"

(a) 马丁："这就是你的书。"

(b) 马丁："这是你的书。"

(c) 马丁："这是你的书吧。"

Language Reference

2 Using 过 to talk about a past experience

The word 过 (guò) comes directly after an action word to indicate that someone has done that thing before. 了 can be used together with 过 (guò) to say that since an action has already been taken, it doesn't need to be done again now (see examples 4 and 5 below).

	Action Word	guò 过		Meaning
1	我	去	过 北京。	I've been to Beijing (before).
2	他没	打	过 乒乓球。	He hasn't played ping pong before.
3	你	去	过 中国吗？	Have you been to China (before)?
4	我已经	吃	过 饭了。	I've already eaten (so I don't need to eat again right now).
5	我给她	送	过 生日礼物了。	I have already given her a birthday gift (so I don't need to give her a gift again right now).

3 Emphasizing what something is or who someone is

就 (jiù) can mean "exactly, precisely." When used this way, 就 (jiù) often comes just before 是 and helps to add emphasis, especially when confirming something that someone else was unsure of or disagreed with.

1 A: 喂？你好，春月在吗？

Hello? Is Isabella there?

B: 你好！我就是春月。
       jiù

Hello! This is Isabella.

2 A: 你看，那个人是大明吗？

Look— is that person Daming?

B: 对，就是他。
    jiù

Yes, that's him.

3 这就是我要送你的礼物。
  jiù

This is exactly the gift that I'm going to give you.

4 A: 我觉得这个题的答案是 B！
        tí   dá'àn

I think the answer to this problem is B!

B: 不对！就是 C！
    jiù

Wrong! It's definitely C!

2d Using the Language `INTERPERSONAL`

Think of a Chinese cultural activity that you know how to say, or refer to the Word Bank below for more options. Ask your classmates whether they have ever done that activity. If they have, did they like it or not? If they have not done that activity before, would they want to or not? Keep track of your classmates' answers and be prepared to report back to the class. Now your teacher will know what aspects of Chinese culture your class is interested in!

Example:

你看过中国电影吗？

WORD BANK

xiě shūfǎ
1 写书法
write Chinese
calligraphy

liàn wǔshù
2 练武术
practice
martial arts

diànshìjù
3 看中国电视剧
watch Chinese TV
dramas

gē
4 听中文歌
listen to Chinese
songs

májiàng
5 打麻将
play mahjong

Zhōngguóchéng
6 去中国城
go to Chinatown

Better and better

3a Language Model   TARGET LANGUAGE INPUT

Your teacher will lead a discussion about the images below. Try to participate as much as you can. If there is anything you don't understand, let your teacher know.

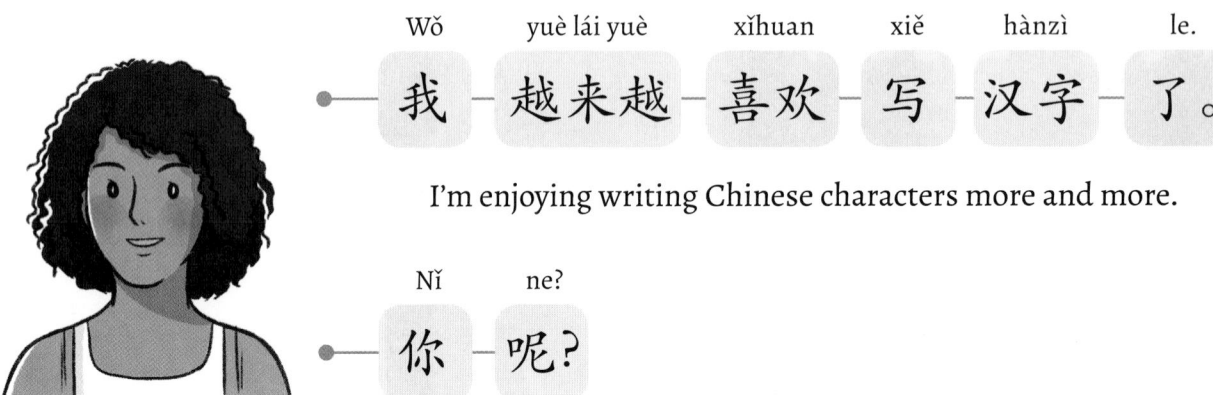

Wǒ	yuè lái yuè	xǐhuan	xiě	hànzì	le.
我	越来越	喜欢	写	汉字	了。

I'm enjoying writing Chinese characters more and more.

Nǐ	ne?
你	呢？

How about you?

1

xiě   hànzì

写汉字

to write Chinese
characters

2

shēngcí

学生词

to learn new
words

3b New Words in Context INTERPRETIVE

Listen to the audio and try to understand as much as you can. Then read the passage, using the pinyin text and vocabulary list to figure out unfamiliar words.

我每天都会学些生词，还经常练习写汉字。
现在我会写的汉字越来越多了。昨天我的
中文老师告诉我，我的发音也越来越好。
我很高兴！我现在越来越喜欢学中文了！

Wǒ měi tiān dōu huì xué xiē shēngcí, hái jīngcháng liànxí xiě hànzì.

Xiànzài wǒ huì xiě de hànzì yuè lái yuè duō le. Zuótiān wǒ de

Zhōngwén lǎoshī gàosù wǒ, wǒ de fāyīn yě yuè lái yuè hǎo.

Wǒ hěn gāoxìng! Wǒ xiànzài yuè lái yuè xǐhuan xué Zhōngwén le!

Comprehension Check

                                                                    T   F

1   Miko studies new vocabulary and Chinese grammar every day.   ○   ○

2   Miko says her Chinese handwriting is getting more and more pretty.   ○   ○

Vocabulary

Audio

	Word	Pinyin	Meaning
14	些	xiē	some, a few
15	生词	shēngcí	new words, vocabulary
16	练习	liànxí	to practice; exercises
17	写	xiě	to write
18	汉字	hànzì	Chinese characters
19	越来越	yuè lái yuè	more and more
20	发音	fāyīn	pronunciation; to pronounce

Complete the exercise below to check your understanding of what you learned in Section 3. If you have questions, consult the Language Reference section.

Rearrange the Chinese words and phrases in each row to translate the English sentences.

1 紧张 | 我 | 越来越 | 了。
I'm getting more and more nervous.

2 越来越 | 的 | 饭 | 好吃。 | 做 | 他
The food he makes tastes better and better.

3 越来越 | 中文 | 好 | 学 | 了。 | 她 | 觉得
She thinks that Chinese is getting easier and easier to learn.

Language Reference •

4 Followed by a verb or descriptive word, 越来越 (yuè lái yuè) describes a change over time. In spoken Chinese, it's very common to add a 了 at the end of a sentence with 越来越 (yuè lái yuè), but it doesn't change the meaning of the sentence.

　　　yuè lái yuè
1 他越来越忙了。
He's getting busier and busier.

　　　　　　　yuè lái yuè
2 老师问的问题越来越难。
The questions the teacher asks are getting more and more difficult.

　　xiě　　　hànzì yuè lái yuè
3 她写的汉字越来越好看了。
The Chinese characters that she writes are getting more and more beautiful.

　　yuè lái yuè
4 我越来越喜欢拉二胡了。
I like playing the erhu more and more.

3d Using the Language INTERPERSONAL

How has your perspective on learning Chinese changed over time? Do you think certain things are getting easier and easier, or harder and harder? Or is there something related to learning Chinese that you are enjoying more and more? In small groups, share one of your opinions with your classmates and ask if they feel the same. Is your perspective a common one among your classmates?

Example:

我觉得中文的语法越来越容易学了。你同意吗?

5Cs
CONNECTIONS
COMMUNITIES
COMMUNICATION
CULTURES
COMPARISONS

汉字 (hànzì) were developed thousands of years ago and, in the past, they were borrowed to serve as a writing system for other languages, including Japanese and Korean. Today, the Japanese writing system still includes many 汉字 (hànzì), which they call kanji, although 汉字 (hànzì) are no longer the only method of Japanese writing. In the 1400s, the Koreans developed an alphabet that is the basis of their written language today, and they now rarely use 汉字 (hànzì).

How many languages are shown in the sign above? Can you guess which languages they are?

Put the Pieces Together!

A Reading and Listening INTERPRETIVE

Passage 1

MARTIN AND MAYA HAVE MET UP AFTER SCHOOL AND ARE PREPARING TO WORK ON HOMEWORK TOGETHER.

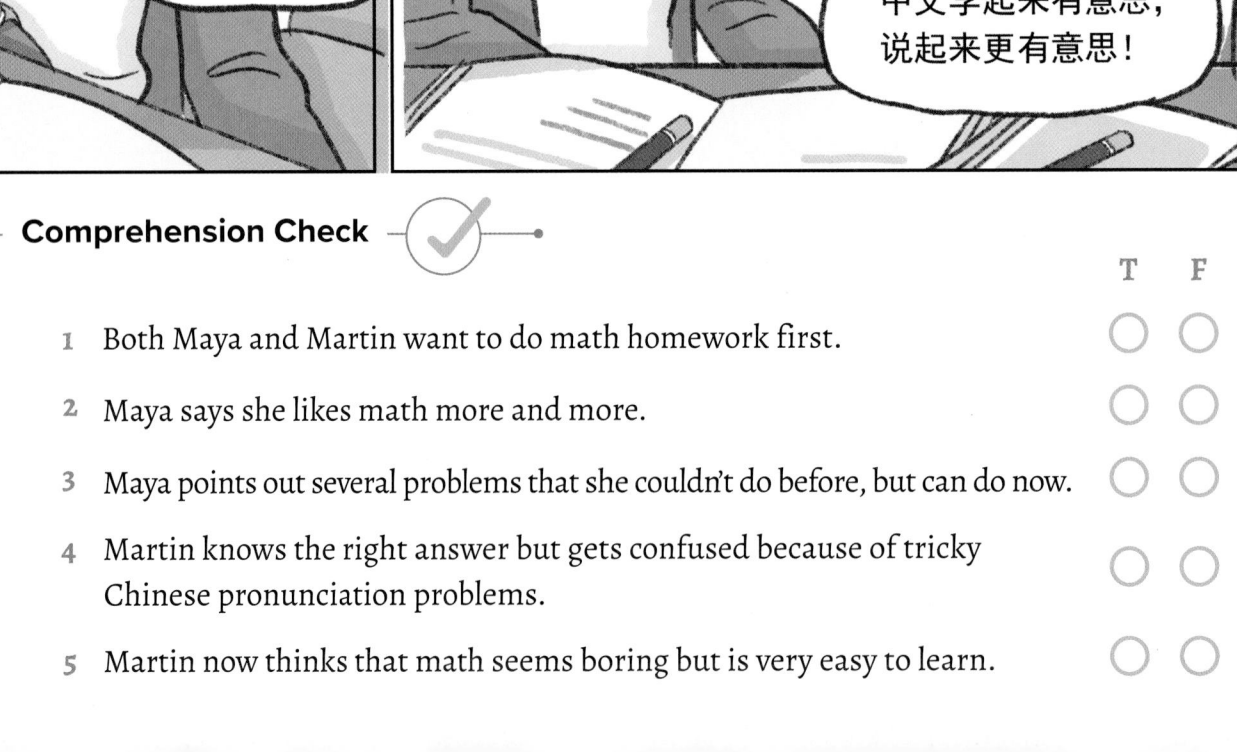

Comprehension Check

		T	F
1	Both Maya and Martin want to do math homework first.	○	○
2	Maya says she likes math more and more.	○	○
3	Maya points out several problems that she couldn't do before, but can do now.	○	○
4	Martin knows the right answer but gets confused because of tricky Chinese pronunciation problems.	○	○
5	Martin now thinks that math seems boring but is very easy to learn.	○	○

Passage 2 Your friend wanted to improve her Chinese pronunciation and bought this book at the bookstore. Do you think she picked the right book?

Passage 3 Listen to the conversation between Miko and Leo, and then answer the following questions.

1 What does Miko say she likes more and more?

  (a) speaking Chinese
  (b) reading Chinese
  (c) writing Chinese

2 In what area does Leo want to improve his Chinese?

  (a) grammar
  (b) character writing
  (c) pronunciation

3 What will Leo help Miko do?

  (a) solve a Chinese grammar problem
  (b) review new vocabulary
  (c) preview tomorrow's lesson

Imagine that you are considering taking an online course. Talk to a partner and ask him/her what he/she thinks of the courses listed below. Does he/she think they would be easy or difficult? Interesting or boring? Be prepared to share your partner's opinions with the rest of the class.

C Final Project PRESENTATIONAL

Academic Fair

Imagine that your class is preparing for an academic fair to help promote your Chinese program to other students. In pairs, use Chinese to create a poster about Chinese class. Possible information to include:

- Cultural information that you have learned
- Reasons why studying Chinese is useful
- A quote from you or your partner about the experience of learning Chinese

Add simple English translations so that your peers who don't know any Chinese can also learn from your poster.

一起学中文吧!
Let's learn Chinese Together!

会说中文的人
越来越多了。

你好
The number of people who can
speak Chinese is growing.

"中文学起来很
有意思!" ~小文
"Learning Chinese
is very interesting!"
-Vanessa

二胡是一种很好听
的中国乐器。
The erhu, a type of Chinese
instrument.

"我已经看过两个
中国电影了！我
觉得中国电影
很好看。" ~天天
"I like watching Chinese
movies!" -Ted

Can-Do Goals

Talk with your teacher if you have questions or if you are not certain you can do the following tasks:

- Explore fun activities to support Chinese learning outside the classroom
- Describe your impression of different activities
- Say that you or others were mistaken in their thinking
- Discuss what you have done before
- Understand when someone emphasizes what something is or who someone is
- Describe how a situation changes over time

Cultural Knowledge

What are some interesting ways to support your Chinese learning?

Elementary students in Hebei Province practicing Chinese calligraphy

School and Activities

Miko: We're having our end-of-semester Chinese Club party this afternoon! Are you guys going to be there?

Martin: Yes, I'll be there! I signed up to play a song on the erhu.

Leo: I'll be there, too!

Miko: Great! Maya is performing, too. She'll be singing a song in Chinese. It should be fun!

Can-Do Goals

In this chapter, you will learn to:

- Name some of the types of student clubs available in Chinese schools
- Discuss joining student clubs
- Understand when others express how well they do something
- Make contrasting statements
- Talk about something you are hoping for

xuéshēng   jùlèbù

学生俱乐部
Student Clubs

While it is common for students in China to spend a lot of time preparing for exams and attending cram schools in their free time, many Chinese schools offer a range of different clubs to give students an opportunity to pursue other interests as well.

A performance by the dance team of Foshan High School in Guangdong Province

Dance

Many schools in China have dance clubs. Street dancing is popular, but other styles, including traditional Chinese dance, are performed, too.

Media

Students interested in broadcasting or journalism may be able to join a school newspaper or radio station. Some schools even have a TV station. School news, music and movie reviews, and interviews of fellow students are just some of the types of content created by these clubs.

Volunteering

Volunteer clubs allow students to give back to their communities by organizing donation drives, helping with environmental protection, serving the elderly, guiding travelers at subway stations, and more. Check out these volunteers planting trees in Luannan, Hebei Province.

By the Numbers

Some schools offer anime clubs, which are just a small part of the Japanese comics and anime craze among young Chinese. A 2018 survey of Chinese people younger than 21 years old found that 52 million had cell phone apps for viewing anime and comics.

Middle Schoolers' Anime-Watching Habits

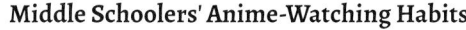
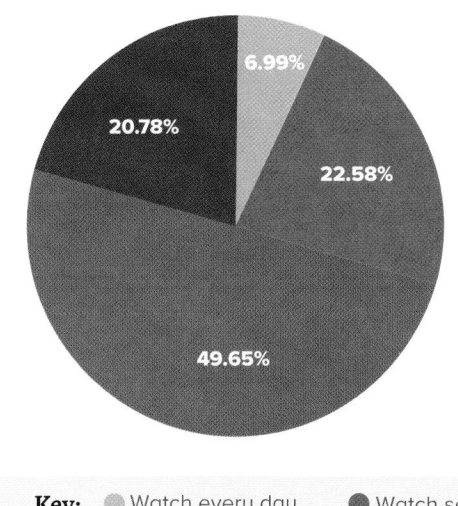

6.99%
20.78%
22.58%
49.65%

High Schoolers' Anime-Watching Habits

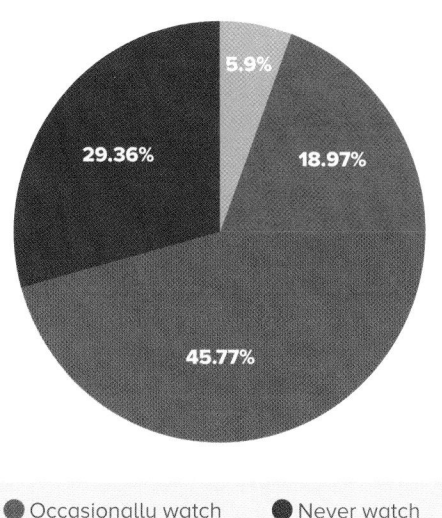

5.9%
29.36%
18.97%
45.77%

Key: ● Watch every day   ● Watch several times a week   ● Occasionally watch   ● Never watch

Sources: Quest Mobile, 2018; guduodata.com, 2018

REFLECT ON THE ESSENTIAL QUESTION

How do you decide what to spend time on outside of class?

1 If you were a student in China, which club mentioned here would you choose to join? Why?

2 What would you want to tell a visiting Chinese student about clubs at your school?

3 Do you think school clubs are important? Why or why not?

Doing things well

1a Language Model TARGET LANGUAGE INPUT

Your teacher will lead a discussion about the image below. Try to participate as much as you can. If there is anything you don't understand, let your teacher know.

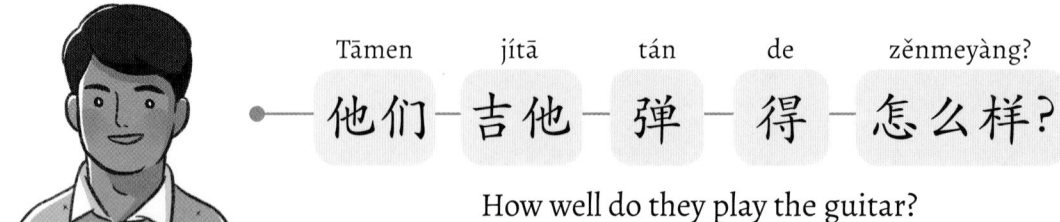

Tāmen	jítā	tán	de	zěnmeyàng?
他们	吉他	弹	得	怎么样?

How well do they play the guitar?

Tā	tán	jítā	tán	de	hěn	hǎo.
她	弹	吉他	弹	得	很	好。

She plays the guitar very well.

Tā	tán	de	bú tài	hǎo.
他	弹	得	不太	好。

He doesn't play (the guitar) well.

Audio

Listen to the audio and try to understand as much as you can. Then read the passage, using the pinyin text and vocabulary list to figure out unfamiliar words.

这个月我加入了中文俱乐部。我在那儿认识了一些新朋友。他们中文说得很好，写汉字也写得很好。最近我经常跟他们一起练习说中文。

Zhège yuè wǒ jiārù le Zhōngwén jùlèbù. Wǒ zài nàr rènshi le

yì xiē xīn péngyou. Tāmen Zhōngwén shuō de hěn hǎo, xiě hànzì yě xiě

de hěn hǎo. Zuìjìn wǒ jīngcháng gēn tāmen yìqǐ liànxí shuō Zhōngwén.

Comprehension Check

		T	F
1	Leo joined Chinese Club this month.	○	○
2	He got to know new friends in the club.	○	○
3	The people in the Chinese club speak Chinese well but are not very good at writing Chinese characters.	○	○

Vocabulary

Audio

	Word	Pinyin	Meaning
1	加入	jiārù	to join
2	俱乐部	jùlèbù	club
3	认识	rènshi	to know (a person), to recognize
4	新	xīn	new
5	得	de	(word used to link a verb to a description of the manner in which it was done)
6	最近	zuìjìn	recently

What a Character!

yán
讠

1 讠   2 讠

The component 讠 (yán) is based on the character 言 (yán), meaning "language." Characters with the 讠 (yán) component often relate to speech.

The school's debate club says it can help students with the following skills. Can you use the pictures to guess each skill? What do you notice about where 讠 (yán) appears in each character?

1
biànlùn
辩论

2
yǎnjiǎng
演讲

3
tǎolùn
讨论

1c Puzzle It Out PROGRESS CHECK

Complete the exercise below to check your understanding of what you learned in Section 1. If you have questions, consult the Language Reference section.

Use the words in the list on the left to complete the translation of each sentence below.

得

的

1 他二胡拉 ⬜ 很好。
He plays the erhu very well.

2 春月是马丁 ⬜ 姐姐。
Isabella is Martin's older sister.

3 她打篮球打 ⬜ 挺好 ⬜ 。
She plays basketball well.

Language Reference

1 Describing the way you do something

As used in this chapter, 得 (de) comes after a verb and connects the verb to a word or phrase that describes how the action is done.

	verb	得	way/degree	
1 你	休息	得	怎么样？	How did you rest?
2 我	休息	得	很好。	I rested very well.
3 他今天	来	得	很早。	He came early today.
4 你	做	得	对！	You did it correctly!

If the sentence contains an object, the sentence is arranged in this way: the verb and its object are stated first, then the verb is repeated followed by the 得 (de) phrase. The first verb may be left out without changing the meaning of the sentence. (In the following examples, the object is shown in a blue box and the verb is shown in a gray box.)

她吹笛子吹^{de}得很好。

她笛子吹^{de}得很好。

She plays the flute very well.

Sometimes, if the thing being discussed is already clear, the speaker may leave out the object, as shown in person B's answer to person A here.

A: 她吹笛子吹^{de}得怎么样？

How is she at playing the flute?

B: 她吹^{de}得很好。

She plays it very well.

Choose one of the student profiles below and keep your choice a secret. Each profile lists some skills that the student learned at a club and can do well. Each profile also lists skills that the student would like to learn from someone else. Circulate around the class, interviewing your classmates to find people who can teach you what you want to learn.

Example:

A: ……我想学踢足球。你足球踢得怎么样？
B: 我加入了足球俱乐部。我足球踢得很好！

A: 太好了！……

俱乐部：
乒乓球俱乐部，
吉他俱乐部

想学：
篮球，二胡，中文

A

俱乐部：
中国乐器俱乐部，足球
俱乐部，数学俱乐部

想学：
吉他，历史，科学

B

俱乐部：
中文俱乐部，网球
俱乐部，历史俱乐部

想学：
乒乓球，数学，古筝

C

俱乐部：
历史俱乐部，篮球
俱乐部，科学俱乐部

想学：
乒乓球，足球，吉他

D

5Cs
CONNECTIONS
COMMUNITIES
COMMUNICATION
COMPARISONS
CULTURES

In both China and the United States, a thumbs-up shows approval, and this gesture is a part of a history of good relations between the two nations. In World War II, American fighter pilots were sent to China to fight against Japan, which had invaded China. Chinese citizens often gave American soldiers a thumbs-up to express their support.

Enjoyable activities

2a Language Model   TARGET LANGUAGE INPUT

Your teacher will lead a discussion about the image below. Try to participate as much as you can. If there is anything you don't understand, let your teacher know.

Tāmen	hěn	xǐhuan	chàng	Zhōngwén	gē.
他们	很	喜欢	唱	中文	歌。

They really like singing Chinese songs.

Mini karaoke booths, each equipped with a karaoke machine, headsets, and microphones, at a train station in the city of Guilin. People use apps to pay to sing songs and receive a recording of their performance that they can share on social media.

2b New Words in Conversation INTERPRETIVE

Listen to the audio and try to understand as much as you can. Then read the dialogue, using the pinyin text and vocabulary list to figure out unfamiliar words.

 我很喜欢唱英文歌和跳中国舞。你觉得我应该加入什么俱乐部？

Wǒ hěn xǐhuan **chàng** Yīngwén **gē** hé **tiào** Zhōngguó **wǔ**. Nǐ juéde wǒ **yīnggāi** jiārù shénme jùlèbù?

 你可以加入我们音乐俱乐部啊！我们经常一起唱歌、跳舞、聊天儿。你可以来跟我们一起玩儿！你想这个星期先跟我们见一面吗？

Nǐ kěyǐ jiārù wǒmen yīnyuè jùlèbù a! Wǒmen jīngcháng yìqǐ **chàng gē**, **tiào wǔ**, **liáo tiānr**. Nǐ kěyǐ lái gēn wǒmen yìqǐ **wánr**! Nǐ xiǎng zhège xīngqī xiān gēn wǒmen **jiàn** yí **miàn** ma?

好啊！听起来很酷！

Hǎo a! Tīng qǐ lái hěn **kù**!

Comprehension Check

		T	F
1	Sanjay likes singing Chinese songs and dancing Chinese-style dances.	○	○
2	According to Maya, in the music club they often dance, chat, and sing together.	○	○
3	Sanjay doesn't seem interested in joining the music club.	○	○

Vocabulary

	Word	Pinyin	Meaning
7	唱歌	chàng gē	to sing (a song)
8	跳舞	tiào wǔ	to dance, to do a (kind of) dance
9	应该	yīnggāi	should, ought to
10	聊天儿	liáo tiānr	to chat

	Word	Pinyin	Meaning
11	玩儿	wánr	to have fun, to play, to hang out
12	见面	jiàn miàn	to meet (up), to meet with
13	酷	kù	cool (meaning: awesome, great)

LANGUAGE CHALLENGE

Chinese has borrowed words from other languages. One example is the word 酷 (kù), meaning "cool." Below are some more examples. Can you match each Chinese word to its image?

1

2

3

4

5

6

bǎolíngqiú
a 保龄球

qiǎokèlì
b 巧克力

shālā
c 沙拉

kǎtōng
d 卡通

kǎolā
e 考拉

pài
f 派

Complete the exercise below to check your understanding of what you learned in Section 2. If you have questions, consult the Language Reference section.

Rearrange the Chinese words and phrases in each row to translate the English sentences.

1 他 ｜ 你 ｜ 跟 ｜ 吗？｜ 过 ｜ 见 ｜ 面
Have you met him before?

2 老师经常 ｜ 教 ｜ 中文 ｜ 我们 ｜ 唱 ｜ 歌。
The teacher often teaches us to sing Chinese songs.

3 喜欢 ｜ 我 ｜ 中国 ｜ 跳 ｜ 舞。｜ 很
I really like doing Chinese dances.

Language Reference ●

2 Verbs that are made up of two words

There are some words in Chinese that usually act as a single verb but are made up of two words — a single-character verb and its single-character object. Examples of this kind of word that you have learned so far include 睡觉, 起床, 上课, 跳舞 (tiào wǔ), 唱歌 (chàng gē), 聊天儿 (liáo tiānr), 见面 (jiàn miàn), 发音, and 请假. Often, descriptions or details are added between the verb and the noun, breaking the word apart.

1 我朋友很喜欢唱英文歌。
(chàng / gē)
My friend really likes to sing English songs.

2 她昨天晚上睡了一个好觉。
She had a good sleep last night. (She slept well last night.)

3 你跳过中国舞吗？
(tiào / wǔ)
Have you done a Chinese-style dance before?

4 我们以前见过面吗？
(jiàn / miàn)
Have we met before?

When 得 (de) is used with this type of word, the single-character verb appears by itself (without the single-character object) directly in front of the 得 (de) phrase.

5 她昨天睡得很晚。

Last night she went to bed really late.

liáo tiānr liáo
6 他们聊天儿聊得很高兴。

They chatted happily. (They really enjoyed their conversation.)

2d Using the Language INTERPERSONAL

Think of two famous performers and discuss them with a partner. Tell your partner what you think of the celebrities' singing and dancing abilities and ask your partner what he/she thinks about their talents. Do you and your partner share the same opinions, or do you have different thoughts on the celebrities' abilities? If you agree with your partner, give that celebrity a thumbs up when commenting.

你觉得……唱歌唱得怎么样?

Contrasting statements

3a Language Model TARGET LANGUAGE INPUT

Your teacher will lead a discussion about the image below. Try to participate as much as you can. If there is anything you don't understand, let your teacher know.

Suīrán	chéngjì	hěn	zhòngyào,
虽然	成绩	很	重要,

Although grades are very important,

dànshì	yǒu	yí	gè	hǎo	xīnqíng
但是	有	一	个	好	心情

(but) having a positive state of mind

yě	hěn	zhòngyào.
也	很	重要。

is also very important.

3b New Words in Context `INTERPRETIVE`

Audio

Listen to the audio and try to understand as much as you can. Then read the email Daming wrote to Martin, using the pinyin text and vocabulary list to figure out unfamiliar words.

马丁，我们学校明天开始放假。我后天会回北京。你这个学期很忙吧？ 虽然我希望你每门课的成绩都很好，但是我更希望你每天的心情都很好。加油吧！我们北京见！

Mǎdīng, wǒmen xuéxiào míngtiān kāishǐ **fàng jià**. Wǒ hòutiān huì **huí** Běijīng. Nǐ zhège **xuéqī** hěn máng ba? **Suīrán** wǒ **xīwàng** nǐ měi mén kè de **chéngjì** dōu hěn hǎo, dànshì wǒ gèng **xīwàng** nǐ měi tiān de xīnqíng dōu hěn hǎo. Jiā yóu ba! Wǒmen Běijīng jiàn!

Comprehension Check

		T	F
1	Daming will return to Beijing for vacation.	○	○
2	Daming hopes that Martin will get good grades.	○	○
3	Daming thinks getting good grades is the most important thing.	○	○

Vocabulary

Audio

	Word	Pinyin	Meaning
14	放假	fàng jià	to have a vacation (or holiday), to have time off
15	回	huí	to return, to go back
16	学期	xuéqī	school term, semester
17	虽然	suīrán	although
18	希望	xīwàng	to hope, to wish; hope
19	成绩	chéngjì	grades, score, achievement

5Cs

COMMUNICATION

COMMUNITIES
CULTURES
CONNECTIONS
COMPARISONS

The semester is ending! Here are some common phrases you may want to use during this time.

If you're talking about grades with a friend and they say they think you did well, you might respond by saying "希望吧！(Xīwàng ba!)," meaning "I hope so!"

As the semester ends, you may want to say goodbye (for now) to classmates and teachers. One way to do so is to say "下个学期见！(Xià gè xuéqī jiàn!)," or "See you next semester!"

To express excitement about the upcoming vacation, you could say "放假了！(Fàng jià le!)," which means (roughly) "It's vacation time!"

3c Puzzle It Out PROGRESS CHECK

Complete the exercise below to check your understanding of what you learned in Section 3.
If you have questions, consult the Language Reference section.

Use the words in the list on the left to complete each sentence below.

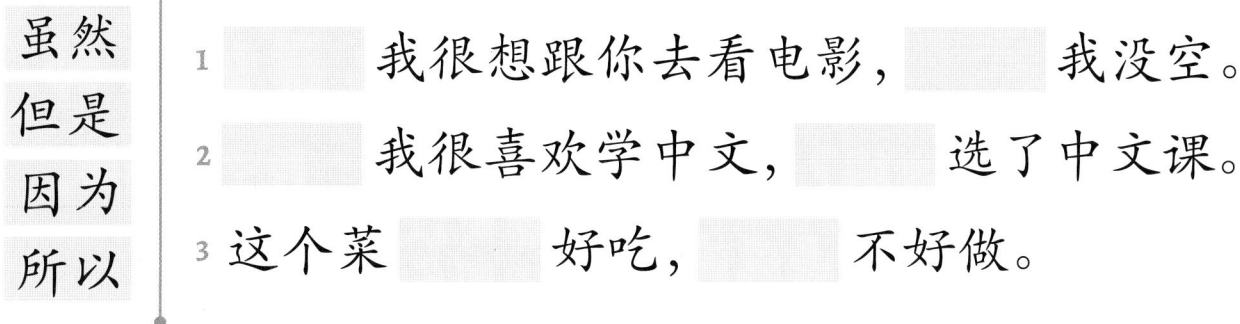

虽然
但是
因为
所以

1 _____ 我很想跟你去看电影，_____ 我没空。

2 _____ 我很喜欢学中文，_____ 选了中文课。

3 这个菜 _____ 好吃，_____ 不好做。

Language Reference

3 Expressing contrasting statements

The word 虽然 (suīrán) is usually followed by 可是 or 但是 later in the sentence. The 虽然 (suīrán)...可是/但是 pattern means that the first statement is somewhat at odds with the one that follows.

suīrán
1 虽然这门课有点儿难，但是选这门课的人很多。
Although this course is a bit hard, there are many people choosing it.

suīrán
2 虽然我很喜欢吃中国菜，但是我不会做中国菜。
Although I really like to eat Chinese food, I don't know how to make Chinese food.

suīrán
3 这件衣服虽然很好看，可是太贵了。
Although this piece of clothing looks very nice, it is too expensive.

In pairs, look at the flyers for the clubs below. Would you like to join any of them? Tell your partner which clubs (if any) you would join and why. Then ask your partner which one(s) he/she wants to join.

 科学俱乐部

你喜欢学科学吗？

你希望你的科学课成绩可以更好吗？

 加入我们吧！

中国乐器俱乐部

如果你会一种中国乐器，你可以加入我们中国乐器俱乐部!

每个星期三、星期四见面

历史俱乐部

历史可以告诉我们很多东西。

你想知道是什么吗？

见面时间：星期二四点

 乒乓球俱乐部

我们每个星期一、三、四、五都会一起打乒乓球。

你一定会比以前打得更好！

Put the Pieces Together!

A Reading and Listening INTERPRETIVE

Audio

Passage 1

MARTIN, LEO, MAYA, AND MIKO ARE ALL ATTENDING THE CHINESE CLUB'S END-OF-SEMESTER CELEBRATION. MAYA HAS JUST FINISHED SINGING A CHINESE SONG.

204

Comprehension Check ✓

		T	F
1	Leo and Martin both think that Maya sings very well.	○	○
2	Everyone is very happy that school vacation is coming.	○	○
3	Martin joined a club and got to know some new friends.	○	○
4	According to Miko, Martin is not happy about school vacation because it means he will not be able to meet up with Maya.	○	○

Passage 2 Based on this ad, guess what this store sells.

a. school supplies   b. pet supplies   c. groceries

新学期

大减价

Passage 3 Listen to the conversation between the girl and the boy. Are the following statements true (T) or false (F)?

		T	F
1	The girl is part of the ping-pong club.	○	○
2	The boy knows the girl's new friend, since they are both part of the guzheng club.	○	○
3	The boy's new friend is an American.	○	○
4	The girl correctly guesses that the boy's new friend is Martin.	○	○

B Speaking INTERPERSONAL

It's the end of the semester! Reflect on your experience and think of two things that you want to do better or do differently next semester. In groups, tell your classmates about these goals for next semester and ask if they hope to do the same. Keep track of everyone's answers and be prepared to tell the rest of the class what the most popular goals in your group are.

Example:

我希望我下个学期每天都能早点儿睡觉。……你呢?

C Final Project — PRESENTATIONAL

Chinese Club Celebration

Step 1: In groups, brainstorm a list of activities that your Chinese club could do as part of an end-of-semester gathering to celebrate Chinese culture. If your group mates mention an idea that you don't think would work, tactfully explain that although you like their idea, you also see a problem with it. Each group should choose three activities that the club could do and decide which of the three you would do first, next, and last.

Example discussion:

A: 我们教老师和同学唱中文歌吧！

B: 虽然唱中文歌很有意思，可是很多人不会说中文。教他们唱中文歌太难了。

Step 2: Work with your group mates to prepare a presentation about your ideas. State which activities you've chosen and why, and give the order in which you plan to do them.

Step 3: As the other groups give their presentations, write down any activities that you would like to do. After the presentations are complete, your teacher will lead a discussion about which activities are the class favorites. Be prepared to share your preferences.

WORD BANK

jiǎn zhǐ
1 剪纸
do paper cutting

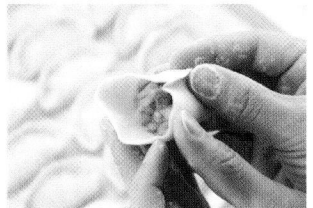

bāo
2 包饺子
make dumplings

shūfǎ
3 写书法
write calligraphy

zhēnzhū nǎichá
4 做珍珠奶茶
make bubble tea

Can-Do Goals

Talk with your teacher if you have questions or if you are not certain you can do the following tasks:

- Name some of the types of student clubs available in Chinese schools
- Discuss joining student clubs
- Understand when others express how well they do something
- Make contrasting statements
- Talk about something you are hoping for

Cultural Knowledge

What are some types of student clubs that can be found in China?

Children in Hebei Province perform a dance

Photo Credits

Every effort has been made to accurately credit the copyright owners of materials reproduced in this publication. Omissions brought to our attention will be corrected in subsequent editions.

Unit 1 Opener

p.1, robinimages2013/Shutterstock.com; **p.2,** Maridav/Shutterstock.com

Chapter 1

p.4, astudio/Shutterstock.com Uwe Aranas/Shutterstock.com; **p.5,** Tom Wang/Shutterstock.com; **p.6,** Nishihama/Shutterstock.com; Dream79/Shutterstock.com; DigitalMammoth/Shutterstock.com; **p.9,** baibaz/Shutterstock.com; Billion Photos/Shutterstock.com; Joe Gough/Shutterstock.com; **p.10,** photos for composite image by BananyakoSensei/Shutterstock.com, XIE WENHUI/Shutterstock.com, Joseph GTK/Shutterstock.com, Alessio Ferreri/Shutterstock.com, and Daniela Josifova/Shutterstock.com; **p.11,** Paul_Brighton/Shutterstock.com; 54613/Shutterstock.com; **p.13,** DedMityay/Shutterstock.com; Ruslan Grechka/Shutterstock.com; BilanolShutterstock.com; **p.15,** Rauf Aliyev/Shutterstock.com; **p.19,** Ryho/Shutterstock.com; sahua d/Shutterstock.com; sahua d/Shutterstock.com; sahua d/Shutterstock.com **p.20,** aphotostory/Shutterstock.com; Mark Zhu/Shutterstock.com; B.Zhou/Shutterstock.com; Rawpixel.com/Shutterstock.com; **p.21,** photo courtesy of Chunmei Guan; **p.22,** Nicolas Maderna/Shutterstock.com

Chapter 2

p.24, Hung Chung Chih/Shutterstock.com; 1828858957/Shutterstock.com; **p.25,** chuyuss/Shutterstock.com; notkoo/Shutterstock.com; Lulupainting/Shutterstock.com; Olga1818/Shutterstock.com; **p.26,** lzfv/Shutterstock.com; superjoseph/Shutterstock.com; Sean Pavone/Shutterstock.com; **p.29,** tong patong/Shutterstock.com; gyn9037/Shutterstock.com; Radiokafka/Shutterstock.com; **p.30,** Tao Jiang/Shutterstock.com; Paolo Costa/Shutterstock.com; Sony Herdiana/Shutterstock.com; **p.31,** Voinau Pavel/Shutterstock.com; **p.34,** Lifestyle Travel Photo/Shutterstock.com; Sean Pavone/Shutterstock.com; fuyu liu/Shutterstock.com; Alexandra Lande/Shutterstock.com; **p.35,** Tyler Olson/Shutterstock.com; WitR/Shutterstock.com; tab62/Shutterstock.com; **p.39,** lisheng2121/Shutterstock.com; Anastasia Boiko/Shutterstock.com; Purich Sophonyossawat/Shutterstock.com; Oliver Hoffmann/Shutterstock.com; **p.40,** humphery/Shutterstock.com; Yuri Yavnik/Shutterstock.com; pixiaomo/Shutterstock.com; Zvonimir Atletic/Shutterstock.com; Alena Charykova/Shutterstock.com; Lawrence Bufalino/Shutterstock.com; Mikhail Semenov/Shutterstock.com; **p.41,** Pixeljoy/Shutterstock.com; photos for composite image by zhao jiankang/Shutterstock.com and Cookie Studio/Shutterstock.com; yuda chen/Shutterstock.com; photos for composite image by 1828858957/Shutterstock.com and Cookie Studio/Shutterstock.com; photos for composite image by Hung Chung Chih/Shutterstock.com and Cookie Studio/Shutterstock.com; **p.42,** chuyuss/Shutterstock.com

Chapter 3

p.44, Pete Niesen/Shutterstock.com; Giusparta/Shutterstock.com; **p. 45,** S_Z/Shutterstock.com; **p.46,** zhao jiankang/Shutterstock.com; Alex Cimbal/Shutterstock.com; **p.49,** illustrations for composite image by magnusz28/Shutterstock.com, cve iv/Shutterstock.com, and Passakorn Umpornmaha/Shutterstock.com; illustrations for composite image by TeraVector/Shutterstock.com, Macrovector/Shutterstock.com, Incomible/Shutterstock.com, nalhcal/Shutterstock.com, and Studio Photo MH/Shutterstock.com; illustrations for composite image by Adam Vilimek/Shutterstock.com, Elnour/Shutterstock.com, Shtonado/Shutterstock.com, Bakhtiar Zein/Shutterstock.com, astudio/Shutterstock.com, and Willee Cole Photography/Shutterstock.com; **p.50,** photos for composite image by Passakorn sakulphan/Shutterstock.com and ESB Professional/Shutterstock.com; **p.51,** photos for composite image by Uwe Aranas/Shutterstock.com and Dilen/Shutterstock.com; **p.54,** andriano.cz/Shutterstock.com; photos for composite image by d13/Shutterstock.com and luceluce/Shutterstock.com; gilead/Shutterstock.com; Halfpoint/Shutterstock.com; **p.55,** zhao jiankang/Shutterstock.com; Yuri Yavnik/Shutterstock.com; Daniel Chetroni/Shutterstock.com; LightField Studios/Shutterstock.com; Sergey Novikov/Shutterstock.com; Suzanne Tucker/Shutterstock.com; Yuganov Konstantin/Shutterstock.com; Rawpixel.com/Shutterstock.com; **p.59,** Yao Moxi/Shutterstock.com; **p.60,** Malchev/Shutterstock.com; Malchev/Shutterstock.com; Malchev/Shutterstock.com;

Malchev/Shutterstock.com; real_content/Shutterstock.com; Khun Ta/Shutterstock.com; Hunter Crenian/Shutterstock.com; Keitma/Shutterstock.com; **p.61**, alphaspirit/Shutterstock.com; LifetimeStock/Shutterstock.com; Singkham/Shutterstock.com; Naypong Studio/Shutterstock.com; Nestor Rizhniak/Shutterstock.com; **p.62**, aphotostory/Shutterstock.com

Unit 2 Opener

p.63, Beliakina Ekaterina/Shutterstock.com; **p.64**, dotshock/Shutterstock.com

Chapter 4

p.66, Brandon Fike/Shutterstock.com; **p.67**, Antoniogut/Shutterstock.com; **p.68**, R. MACKAY PHOTOGRAPHY, LLC/Shutterstock.com; Monkey Business Images/Shutterstock.com; **p.70**, Vtmila/Shutterstock.com; **p.72**, Brocreative/Shutterstock.com; **p.74**, junrong/Shutterstock.com; **p.75**, Comaniciu Dan/Shutterstock.com; Brian A Jackson/Shutterstock.com; **p.76**, photos for composite image by Pavel Shlykov/Shutterstock.com, rnl/Shutterstock.com, and Mego studio/Shutterstock.com; **p.79**, William Perugini/Shutterstock.com; Avesun/Shutterstock.com; Supa Chan/Shutterstock.com; **p.80**, Krakenimages.com/Shutterstock.com; Krakenimages.com/Shutterstock.com; Krakenimages.com/Shutterstock.com; Krakenimages.com/Shutterstock.com; fizkes/Shutterstock.com; fizkes/Shutterstock.com; fizkes/Shutterstock.com; fizkes/Shutterstock.com; WAYHOME studio/Shutterstock.com; WAYHOME studio/Shutterstock.com; WAYHOME studio/Shutterstock.com; WAYHOME studio/Shutterstock.com; Cookie Studio/Shutterstock.com; Cookie Studio/Shutterstock.com; Cookie Studio/Shutterstock.com; Cookie Studio/Shutterstock.com; **p.84**, photos for composite image by SFIO CRACHO/Shutterstock.com and Elena Nayashkova/Shutterstock.com; Daniela Pelazza/Shutterstock.com; Daniela Pelazza/Shutterstock.com; Kostsov/Shutterstock.com; Dima Moroz/Shutterstock.com; **p.85**, Apostrophe/Shutterstock.com; BrunoRosa/Shutterstock.com; **p.86**, humphery/Shutterstock.com

Chapter 5

p.88, B.Zhou/Shutterstock.com; Brandon Fike/Shutterstock.com; **p.89**, B.Zhou/Shutterstock.com; **p.90**, Anatoliy Karlyuk/Shutterstock.com; GP Studio/Shutterstock.com; Elnur/Shutterstock.com; **p.92**, ra2 studio/Shutterstock.com; estherpoon/Shutterstock.com; Hurst Photo/Shutterstock.com; **p.94**, eurobanks/Shutterstock.com; **p.95**, Doucefleur/Shutterstock.com; Pressmaster/Shutterstock.com; **p.97**, jianbing Lee/Shutterstock.com; **p.99**, Elnur/Shutterstock.com; **p.100**, denio109/Shutterstock.com; **p.102**, Jemastock/Shutterstock.com; Blan-k/Shutterstock.com; bonchan/Shutterstock.com; **p.109**, pattern for composite image by Sunspire/Shutterstock.com; **p.110**, Brandon Fike/Shutterstock.com

Chapter 6

p.112, ch_ch/Shutterstock.com; **p.113**, PETER PARKS/AFP via Getty Images; **p.114**, Rawpixel.com/Shutterstock.com; Volurol/Shutterstock.com; **p.117**, Dean Drobot/Shutterstock.com; **p.119**, Antonio Guillem/Shutterstock.com; fizkes/Shutterstock.com; Mila Davidovic/Shutterstock.com; Nutlegal Photographer/Shutterstock.com; **p.121**, Kabardins photo/Shutterstock.com; New Africa/Shutterstock.com; aastock/Shutterstock.com; **p.123**, Jaroslav Machacek/Shutterstock.com; Mimma Key/Shutterstock.com; **p.124**, nuddss/Shutterstock.com; **p.127**, Cookie Studio/Shutterstock.com; aslysun/Shutterstock.com; 9nong/Shutterstock.com; **p.132**, Dragon_Fly/Shutterstock.com; Antonio Guillem/Shutterstock.com; fizkes/Shutterstock.com; OneStockPhoto/Shutterstock.com; pathdoc/Shutterstock.com; carballo/Shutterstock.com; fizkes/Shutterstock.com; Simone van den Berg/Shutterstock.com; **p.133**, Vitalliy/Shutterstock.com; **p.134**, Icatnews/Shutterstock.com

Unit 3 Opener

p.135, Jack.Q/Shutterstock.com; **p.136**, Ollyy/Shutterstock.com

Chapter 7

p.138, Wang Sing/Shutterstock.com; kan_chana/Shutterstock.com; **p.139**, sirikorn thamniyom/Shutterstock.com; **p.140**, Just dance/Shutterstock.com; **p.143**, Khosro/Shutterstock.com; **p.144**, photos for composite image by Visual Generation/Shutterstock.com, Beresnev/Shutterstock.com, Mochipet/Shutterstock.com, and DenysHolovatiuk/Shutterstock.com; **p.145**, Jacob Lund/Shutterstock.com; Rawpixel.com/Shutterstock.com; **p.148**, Yulai Studio/Shutterstock.com; Concept Photo/Shutterstock.com; BaLL LunLa/Shutterstock.com; Pressmaster/Shutterstock.com; Paulo Vilela/Shutterstock.com; Dmytro Zinkevych/Shutterstock.com; **p.149**, Dimedrol68/Shutterstock.com; **p.150**,

Dean Drobot/Shutterstock.com; Elnur/Shutterstock.com; **p.152,** Asier Romero/Shutterstock.com; **p.154,** Monkey Business Images/Shutterstock.com; **p.159,** Kekyalyaynen/Shutterstock.com; Rawpixel.com/Shutterstock.com; Josep Suria/Shutterstock.com; Lisa F. Young/Shutterstock.com; Dragon Images/Shutterstock.com; fizkes/Shutterstock.com; **p.160,** Africa Studio/Shutterstock.com

Chapter 8

p.162, 54613/Shutterstock.com; zhangjin_net/Shutterstock.com; **p.163,** TonyV3112/Shutterstock.com; **p.164,** kiyechka53/Shutterstock.com; **p.167,** Krakenimages.com/Shutterstock.com; Zastolskiy Victor/Shutterstock.com; maroke/Shutterstock.com; Linda_K/Shutterstock.com; **p.168,** smolaw/Shutterstock.com; Have a nice day Photo/Shutterstock.com; **p.170,** wavebreakmedia/Shutterstock.com; **p.173,** koi88/Shutterstock.com; TunedIn by Westend61/Shutterstock.com; Gima Yuzuru/Shutterstock.com; aslysun/Shutterstock.com; Axel Bueckert/Shutterstock.com; aphotostory/Shutterstock.com; **p.174,** michaeljung/Shutterstock.com; PR Image Factory/Shutterstock.com; **p.177,** ImagingL/Shutterstock.com; **p.182,** Lukas Hlavac/Shutterstock.com; Quality Stock Arts/Shutterstock.com; Dean Drobot/Shutterstock.com; ABO PHOTOGRAPHY/Shutterstock.com; red mango/Shutterstock.com; ESB Professional/Shutterstock.com; **p.183,** photos for composite image by XiXinXing/Shutterstock.com, BlackMac/Shutterstock.com, and TuiPhotoEngineer/Shutterstock.com; **p.184,** junrong/Shutterstock.com

Chapter 9

p.186, windmoon/Shutterstock.com; Riderfoot/Shutterstock.com; **p.187,** chinahbzyg/Shutterstock.com; **p.188,** UfaBizPhoto/Shutterstock.com; **p.190,** Stock_VectorSale/Shutterstock.com; tmcphotos/Shutterstock.com; VGstockstudio/Shutterstock.com; **p.192,** musmellow/Shutterstock.com; **p.193,** StreetVJ/Shutterstock.com; **p.195,** Dusan Zidar/Shutterstock.com; Andrey_Popov/Shutterstock.com; Mindscape studio/Shutterstock.com; nelea33/Shutterstock.com; gresei/Shutterstock.com; Yatra/Shutterstock.com; **p.197,** Dmitry Lobanov/Shutterstock.com; **p.198,** Sumala Chidchoi/Shutterstock.com; **p.200,** Art_Photo/Shutterstock.com; **p.202,** Palsur/Shutterstock.com; Duc Mityagov photographer/Shutterstock.com; photos for composite image by Hurst Photo/Shutterstock.com, kontur-vid/Shutterstock.com, and Jiri Hera/Shutterstock.com; **p.206,** Mickicev Atelje/Shutterstock.com; **p.207,** zhaoliang70/Shutterstock.com; fotohunter/Shutterstock.com; leungchopan/Shutterstock.com; mama_mia/Shutterstock.com; **p.208,** jianbing Lee/Shutterstock.com

Vocabulary Index (Chinese – English)

The Chinese–English Vocabulary Index is alphabetized according to pinyin. Words containing the same first Chinese character are grouped together. Words with the same pinyin spelling are organized according to their tone (that is, first tones first, second tones second, third tones third, fourth tones fourth, and neutral tones last). For reference, words introduced in Level 1A of *Go Far with Chinese* appear in this chart. The page numbers of these words are given in brackets.

Chinese	Pinyin	English	Page
		A	
啊	a	(word added at the end of a sentence to add emphasis or excitement)	[1A 137]
奥运会	àoyùnhuì	the Olympic Games	52
		B	
八	bā	eight	[1A 19]
爸爸	bàba	father, dad	[1A 57]
吧	ba	(word added at the end of a sentence to make a suggestion or to soften the tone)	[1A 137]
半	bàn	half, half an hour	91
帮	bāng	to help	151
包子	bāozi	baozi	7
北京	Běijīng	Beijing	[1A 89]
本	běn	(measure word for books)	[1A 186]
比	bǐ	compared with	52
比赛	bǐsài	game, match, competition	[1A 118]
别	bié	don't (in advice or a command)	151
不太	bú tài	not really, not very	[1A 62]

Chinese	Pinyin	English	Page
不用	búyòng	don't need to, don't have to	96
不	bù	no, not	[1A 21]
C			
才	cái	not until, only then	91
菜	cài	a dish (of food); cuisine; vegetables	[1A 205]
长城	Chángchéng	the Great Wall	27
场	chǎng	outdoor court or field (for sports)	[1A 114]
唱歌	chàng gē	to sing (a song)	194
成绩	chéngjì	grades, score, achievement	199
吃	chī	to eat	[1A 205]
迟到	chídào	to be late, to arrive late	151
宠物	chǒngwù	pet (animal)	[1A 67]
吹	chuī	to blow, to play	[1A 133]
错	cuò	wrong, incorrect	169
D			
答案	dá'àn	answer	169
打	dǎ	to hit, to play (basketball, ping-pong)	[1A 109]
打电话	dǎ diànhuà	to make a phone call	[1A 205]
但是	dànshì	but, however	165
的	de	(a connecting word used in possessive and descriptive phrases)	[1A 31]
得	de	(word used to link a verb to a description of the manner in which it was done)	189
得	děi	must, have to, need to	96

Chinese	Pinyin	English	Page
笛子	dízi	flute	[1A 133]
弟弟	dìdi	younger brother	[1A 57]
点	diǎn	to order (food)	[1A 205]
点	diǎn	o'clock (literally, dot or point)	91
店	diàn	store, shop	[1A 137]
电视	diànshì	television	[1A 62]
电影	diànyǐng	movie, motion picture	[1A 158]
东西	dōngxi	thing(s)	151
懂	dǒng	to understand	165
都	dōu	all, both	[1A 84]
对	duì	right, correct	[1A 84]
多	duō	many, much, lots	[1A 216]
E			
饿	è	hungry	120
而且	érqiě	and also	[1A 186]
二	èr	two	[1A 18]
二胡	èrhú	erhu	[1A 133]
二十一	èrshíyī	twenty-one	[1A 163]
F			
发烧	fā shāo	to have a fever	125
发音	fāyīn	pronunciation; to pronounce	175
饭	fàn	meal, cooked rice	12
饭馆	fànguǎn	restaurant	[1A 212]

Chinese	Pinyin	English	Page
放假	fàng jià	to have a vacation (or holiday), to have time off	199
分	fēn	minute	91
份	fèn	(measure word for plates of food)	[1A 212]
复习	fùxí	to review, to study (materials already taught)	146

		G	
感冒	gǎnmào	common cold; to have a cold, to catch a cold	125
高兴	gāoxìng	happy, pleased	77
告诉	gàosu	to tell	146
哥哥	gēge	older brother	[1A 57]
个	gè	(measure word for people and many everyday objects)	[1A 57]
给	gěi	to give; for, to	[1A 205]
跟	gēn	with, and; to	102
更	gèng	even more	52
狗	gǒu	dog	[1A 67]
古筝	gǔzhēng	guzheng	[1A 133]
故宫	Gùgōng	the Forbidden City	27
馆	guǎn	indoor court or field (for playing sports)	[1A 118]
贵	guì	expensive	[1A 186]
过	guò	(word used after a verb to indicate a past experience)	169

		H	
还	hái	also, in addition, too, as well	12
还	hái	still, yet	141

Chinese	Pinyin	English	Page
还是	háishi	or (in questions)	[1A 89]
汉字	hànzì	Chinese characters	175
好	hǎo	fine, good, nice; OK, it's settled	[1A 21]
好吃	hǎochī	tasy, delicious	[1A 205]
好看	hǎokàn	good-looking, nice-looking (used for people and things)	[1A 191]
好玩儿	hǎowánr	fun	32
号	hào	day of the month	[1A 163]
喝	hē	to drink	115
和	hé	and	[1A 41]
很	hěn	very, really	[1A 62]
红烧	hóngshāo	to braise in soy sauce (to red-cook)	[1A 212]
后天	hòutiān	the day after tomorrow	[1A 158]
回	huí	to return, to go back	199
会	huì	can, know how to	[1A 109]
会	huì	will	151
火锅	huǒguō	hot pot	12
J			
吉他	jítā	guitar	[1A 133]
几	jǐ	how many	[1A 57]
计划	jìhuà	plan; to plan	146
家	jiā	home	[1A 94]
加入	jiārù	to join	189
加油	jiā yóu	Do your best! Go! (shouted to cheer players on, literally means "add fuel")	[1A 118]

Chinese	Pinyin	English	Page
简单	jiǎndān	simple	[1A 186]
见	jiàn	to meet with, to see	[1A 182]
见面	jiàn miàn	to meet (up), to meet with	195
件	jiàn	(measure word for clothing)	[1A 191]
教	jiāo	to teach	[1A 141]
饺子	jiǎozi	dumplings (with vegetable and/or meat filling)	[1A 212]
叫	jiào	to be called	[1A 31]
节	jié	festival, holiday	52
姐姐	jiějie	older sister	[1A 57]
今天	jīntiān	today	[1A 158]
紧张	jǐnzhāng	nervous, anxious	77
经常	jīngcháng	frequently, often	[1A 118]
景点	jǐngdiǎn	tourist attraction/site, scenic spot	27
九	jiǔ	nine	[1A 19]
就	jiù	precisely, exactly	169
俱乐部	jùlèbù	club	189
觉得	juéde	to feel, to think	[1A 114]
K			
开始	kāishǐ	to start, to begin; beginning	91
看	kàn	to look at, to watch, to read, to see	[1A 62]
烤鸭	kǎoyā	roast duck	12
科学	kēxué	science	69
渴	kě	thirsty	120

Chinese	Pinyin	English	Page
可是	kěshì	but	[1A 62]
可以	kěyǐ	can, could, may	[1A 141]
课	kè	course, class, lesson	69
客气	kèqi	polite; to be polite/courteous	169
酷	kù	cool (meaning: awesome, great)	195
快乐	kuàilè	happy	[1A 216]
		L	
拉	lā	to pull, to play	[1A 133]
来	lái	to come	125
篮球	lánqiú	basketball (the game and the object)	[1A 109]
老师	lǎoshī	teacher	[1A 21]
了	le	(a word that indicates an action is complete)	[1A 212]
累	lèi	tired, tiring	96
冷	lěng	cold	120
李	Lǐ	Li (surname, sometimes spelled Lee)	[1A 141]
礼物	lǐwù	gift	[1A 168]
历史	lìshǐ	history	73
练习	liànxí	to practice; exercises	175
两	liǎng	two (used when counting things)	[1A 59]
聊天儿	liáo tiānr	to chat	194
林春月	Lín Chūnyuè	Isabella Lopez (a person's name)	[1A 37]
林马丁	Lín Mǎdīng	Martin Lopez (a person's name)	[1A 37]
六	liù	six	[1A 19]

Chinese	Pinyin	English	Page
六月	liùyuè	June	[1A 163]
M			
吗	ma	(question word)	[1A 21]
妈妈	māma	mother, mom	[1A 57]
买	mǎi	to buy	[1A 137]
卖	mài	to sell	[1A 137]
忙	máng	busy	96
猫	māo	cat	[1A 67]
没有	méiyǒu	to not have	[1A 37]
每	měi	every, each	96
美国	Měiguó	United States of America	[1A 84]
妹妹	mèimei	younger sister	[1A 57]
门	mén	(measure word for a course)	69
面条	miàntiáo	noodles	[1A 212]
明天	míngtiān	tomorrow	[1A 158]
名字	míngzi	name	[1A 31]
N			
哪	nǎ	which	69
哪儿	nǎr	where	[1A 94]
那	nà	that	[1A 89]
那	nà	in that case, then, so	[1A 168]
那儿	nàr	there, over there	[1A 114]
难	nán	difficult	[1A 186]

Chinese	Pinyin	English	Page
呢	ne	(word added at the end of a sentence to ask a follow-up question or to ask a question back to someone)	[1A 137]
能	néng	can, to be able	115
你	nǐ	you	[1A 21]
你好	nǐ hǎo	hello	[1A 21]
你们	nǐmen	you (plural)	[1A 41]
鸟巢	Niǎocháo	the Bird's Nest	47
P			
跑步	pǎo bù	to go running; running	47
朋友	péngyou	friend	[1A 41]
便宜	piányi	cheap, inexpensive	[1A 186]
乒乓球	pīngpāngqiú	ping-pong, table tennis; ping-pong ball	[1A 109]
Q			
七	qī	seven	[1A 19]
起床	qǐ chuáng	to get up, to get out of bed	91
起来	qǐ lái	(word that follows a verb and is used to introduce an impression)	165
请假	qǐng jià	to ask for time off, to ask to be excused from (school, work)	115
去	qù	to go	[1A 114]
R			
然后	ránhòu	and then	141
热	rè	hot	120
人	rén	person, people	[1A 84]

Chinese	Pinyin	English	Page
认识	rènshi	to know (a person), to recognize	189
容易	róngyì	easy	165
肉	ròu	meat (frequently pork)	[1A 212]
如果	rúguǒ	if	151
		S	
三	sān	three	[1A 18]
上课	shàng kè	to go to a class, to begin a class, to be in class	74
上午	shàngwǔ	morning (before noon)	[1A 182]
少	shǎo	few, not many, less	146
谁	shéi	who	[1A 37]
什么	shénme	what	[1A 31]
生病	shēng bìng	to get sick	125
生词	shēngcí	new words, vocabulary	175
生日	shēngrì	birthday	[1A 163]
十	shí	ten	[1A 19]
时候	shíhou	(a point in) time, moment	102
时间	shíjiān	time	96
是	shì	to be	[1A 21]
事	shì	thing, matter, something to do	[1A 182]
收拾	shōushi	to pack (up), to tidy (up), to put things away	151
书	shū	book	[1A 62]
舒服	shūfu	comfortable	120
数学	shùxué	math	69

Chinese	Pinyin	English	Page
水	shuǐ	water	115
水果	shuǐguǒ	fruit	7
水立方	Shuǐlìfāng	the Water Cube	47
睡觉	shuì jiào	to sleep	91
说	shuō	to say, to speak	73
四	sì	four	[1A 18]
送	sòng	to give (a gift)	[1A 191]
虽然	suīrán	although	199
所以	suǒyǐ	so, therefore	[1A 216]
T			
他	tā	he, him	[1A 37]
他们	tāmen	they, them (if anyone in the group is male)	[1A 41]
她	tā	she, her	[1A 37]
她们	tāmen	they, them (if everyone in the group is female)	[1A 41]
它	tā	it (used for animals and things)	[1A 67]
太	tài	too, extremely, overly	32
弹	tán	to strum, to pluck, to play	[1A 133]
疼	téng	-ache, aching	125
踢	tī	to kick, to play (soccer)	[1A 109]
题	tí	question, problem (in homework or on a test)	169
天	tiān	day	96
天坛	Tiāntán	Temple of Heaven	27
跳舞	tiào wǔ	to dance, to do a (kind of) dance	194

Chinese	Pinyin	English	Page
听	tīng	to listen to, to hear	[1A 141]
挺	tǐng	quite, fairly, pretty, rather	77
同学	tóngxúe	classmate	[1A 37]
同意	tóngyì	to agree	[1A 191]
头	tóu	head	125

W

Chinese	Pinyin	English	Page
完	wán	to finish, to complete	146
玩儿	wánr	to have fun, to play, to hang out	195
晚	wǎn	late	115
晚上	wǎnshàng	night, evening	[1A 182]
网球	wǎngqiú	tennis; tennis ball	[1A 109]
喂	wéi	hello (over the phone)	[1A 182]
为什么	wèishénme	why	[1A 216]
文学	wénxué	literature	73
问	wèn	to ask (a question)	[1A 168]
问题	wèntí	problem, question	141
我	wǒ	I, me	[1A 21]
我们	wǒmen	we, us	[1A 41]
无聊	wúliáo	boring, bored	32
五	wǔ	five	[1A 19]

X

Chinese	Pinyin	English	Page
希望	xīwàng	to hope, to wish; hope	199
喜欢	xǐhuan	to like	[1A 62]

Chinese	Pinyin	English	Page
下个	xià ge	next	[1A 163]
下午	xiàwǔ	afternoon	[1A 182]
先	xiān	first	141
现在	xiànzài	now, at this time	[1A 94]
想	xiǎng	to want (to do something)	[1A 114]
小明	Xiǎomíng	(a name)	[1A 67]
小区	xiǎoqū	neighborhood, apartment complex	[1A 94]
些	xiē	some, a few	175
写	xiě	to write	175
谢谢	xièxie	thank you, thanks	[1A 141]
新	xīn	new	189
心情	xīnqíng	mood, state of mind	77
星期	xīngqī	week	[1A 94]
星期五	xīngqīwǔ	Friday	[1A 158]
休息	xiūxi	to rest, to take a break	120
选	xuǎn	to choose	73
学	xué	to learn, to study	[1A 84]
学期	xuéqī	school term, semester	199
学生	xúeshēng	student	[1A 21]
学习	xuéxí	studies; to study, to learn	146
学校	xuéxiào	school	[1A 94]

Y

Chinese	Pinyin	English	Page
颜色	yánsè	color	[1A 191]

Chinese	Pinyin	English	Page
要	yào	to be going to (do something), to want (something; to do something)	[1A 182]
也	yě	also, too, as well as	[1A 41]
一	yī	one	[1A 18]
一定	yídìng	certainly, definitely	[1A 168]
一样	yíyàng	same, alike; as…as	102
(一)点儿	(yì)diǎnr	a bit, a little, some	115
一起	yìqǐ	together	102
衣服	yīfu	clothing	[1A 191]
已经	yǐjīng	already	102
以前	yǐqián	before, ago	165
以为	yǐwéi	to mistakenly think, to assume incorrectly	165
因为	yīnwèi	because	[1A 216]
音乐	yīnyuè	music	[1A 141]
应该	yīnggāi	should, ought to	194
英文	Yīngwén	English (language)	[1A 31]
游泳	yóu yǒng	to swim; swimming	47
有	yǒu	to have	[1A 37]
有	yǒu	there is, there are	[1A 114]
有的	yǒude	some	102
有空	yǒu kòng	to have free time, to be free	[1A 158]
有意思	yǒuyìsi	interesting, fun	[1A 114]
又	yòu	again	141

Chinese	Pinyin	English	Page
语法	yǔfǎ	grammar	165
玉米片	yùmǐpiàn	cornflakes	7
预习	yùxí	to preview, to study (materials not yet taught in class)	146
月	yuè	month, moon	[1A 163]
越来越	yuè lái yuè	more and more	175
乐器	yuèqì	musical instrument	[1A 133]
运动	yùndòng	sports, exercise	[1A 118]
Z			
在	zài	to be at, to be in (a place)	[1A 94]
在	zài	at, in	[1A 118]
再	zài	again; then	141
再见	zàijiàn	goodbye, see you again	[1A 21]
早	zǎo	early	115
早上	zǎoshàng	early morning (until about 9:00 a.m.)	[1A 182]
怎么样	zěnmeyàng	How is…?; How about it? Is it OK? How does that sound?	77
这	zhè	this	[1A 89]
这儿	zhèr	here, over here	[1A 114]
只	zhī	(measure word for some animals)	[1A 67]
知道	zhīdào	to know	[1A 89]
中国	Zhōngguó	China	[1A 84]
中文	Zhōngwén	Chinese (language)	[1A 31]
中午	zhōngwǔ	noon	[1A 182]

Chinese	Pinyin	English	Page
种	zhǒng	(measure word for kinds, sorts, types)	[1A 205]
重要	zhòngyào	important	74
周末	zhōumò	weekend	[1A 163]
主意	zhǔyi	idea	[1A 168]
祝	zhù	to wish (well)	[1A 216]
足球	zúqiú	soccer; soccer ball	[1A 109]
最	zuì	most, -est	69
最后	zuìhòu	final, last; finally, lastly	141
最近	zuìjìn	recently	189
昨天	zuótiān	yesterday	[1A 212]
做	zuò	to do, to make	[1A 118]
做菜	zuòcài	to make a dish (of food)	[1A 205]
作业	zuòyè	homework	91

Vocabulary Index (English – Chinese)

The English – Chinese Vocabulary Index is organized based on the alphabetical order of the English definitions. For reference, words introduced in Level 1A of *Go Far with Chinese* appear in this chart. The page numbers of these words are given in brackets.

English	Chinese	Pinyin	Page
A			
-ache, aching	疼	téng	125
afternoon	下午	xiàwǔ	[1A 182]
again	又	yòu	141
again; then	再	zài	141
to agree	同意	tóngyì	[1A 191]
all, both	都	dōu	[1A 84]
already	已经	yǐjīng	102
also, in addition, too, as well	还	hái	12
also, too, as well as	也	yě	[1A 41]
although	虽然	suīrán	199
and	和	hé	[1A 41]
and also	而且	érqiě	[1A 186]
and then	然后	ránhòu	141
answer	答案	dá'àn	169
to ask (a question)	问	wèn	[1A 168]
to ask for time off, to ask to be excused from (school, work)	请假	qǐng jià	115
at, in	在	zài	[1A 118]

English	Chinese	Pinyin	Page
	B		
baozi	包子	bāozi	7
basketball (the game and the object)	篮球	lánqiú	[1A 109]
to be	是	shì	[1A 21]
to be at, to be in (a place)	在	zài	[1A 94]
to be called	叫	jiào	[1A 31]
to be going to (do something), to want (something; to do something)	要	yào	[1A 182]
to be late, to arrive late	迟到	chídào	151
because	因为	yīnwèi	[1A 216]
before, ago	以前	yǐqián	165
Beijing	北京	Běijīng	[1A 89]
the Bird's Nest	鸟巢	Niǎocháo	47
birthday	生日	shēngrì	[1A 163]
a bit, a little, some	(一)点儿	(yì)diǎnr	115
to blow, to play	吹	chuī	[1A 133]
book	书	shū	[1A 62]
boring, bored	无聊	wúliáo	32
to braise in soy sauce (to red-cook)	红烧	hóngshāo	[1A 212]
busy	忙	máng	96
but	可是	kěshì	[1A 62]
but, however	但是	dànshì	165
to buy	买	mǎi	[1A 137]

English	Chinese	Pinyin	Page
C			
can, to be able	能	néng	115
can, could, may	可以	kěyǐ	[1A 141]
can, know how to	会	huì	[1A 109]
cat	猫	māo	[1A 67]
certainly, definitely	一定	yídìng	[1A 168]
to chat	聊天儿	liáo tiānr	194
cheap, inexpensive	便宜	piányi	[1A 186]
China	中国	Zhōngguó	[1A 84]
Chinese characters	汉字	hànzì	175
Chinese (language)	中文	Zhōngwén	[1A 31]
to choose	选	xuǎn	73
classmate	同学	tóngxúe	[1A 37]
clothing	衣服	yīfu	[1A 191]
club	俱乐部	jùlèbù	189
cold	冷	lěng	120
color	颜色	yánsè	[1A 191]
to come	来	lái	125
comfortable	舒服	shūfu	120
common cold; to have a cold, to catch a cold	感冒	gǎnmào	125
compared with	比	bǐ	52
(a connecting word used in possessive and descriptive phrases)	的	de	[1A 31]
cool (meaning: awesome, great)	酷	kù	195

English	Chinese	Pinyin	Page
cornflakes	玉米片	yùmǐpiàn	7
course, class, lesson	课	kè	69
D			
Daming Bai (a person's name)	白大明	Bái Dàmíng	[1A 31]
to dance, to do a (kind of) dance	跳舞	tiào wǔ	194
day	天	tiān	96
the day after tomorrow	后天	hòutiān	[1A 158]
day of the month	号	hào	[1A 163]
difficult	难	nán	[1A 186]
a dish (of food); cuisine; vegetables	菜	cài	[1A 205]
to do, to make	做	zuò	[1A 118]
Do your best! Go! (shouted to cheer players on, literally means "add fuel")	加油	jiā yóu	[1A 118]
dog	狗	gǒu	[1A 67]
don't (in advice or a command)	别	bié	151
don't need to, don't have to	不用	búyòng	96
to drink	喝	hē	115
dumplings (with vegetable and/or meat filling)	饺子	jiǎozi	[1A 212]
E			
early	早	zǎo	115
early morning (until about 9:00 a.m.)	早上	zǎoshàng	[1A 182]
easy	容易	róngyì	165
to eat	吃	chī	[1A 205]
eight	八	bā	[1A 19]

English	Chinese	Pinyin	Page
English (language)	英文	Yīngwén	[1A 31]
erhu	二胡	èrhú	[1A 133]
even more	更	gèng	52
every, each	每	měi	96
expensive	贵	guì	[1A 186]
F			
famous, well-known	有名	yǒumíng	32
father, dad	爸爸	bàba	[1A 57]
to feel, to think	觉得	juéde	[1A 114]
festival, holiday	节	jié	52
few, not many, less	少	shǎo	146
final, last; finally, lastly	最后	zuìhòu	141
fine, good, nice; OK, it's settled	好	hǎo	[1A 21]
to finish, to complete	完	wán	146
first	先	xiān	141
five	五	wǔ	[1A 19]
flute	笛子	dízi	[1A 133]
the Forbidden City	故宫	Gùgōng	27
four	四	sì	[1A 18]
frequently, often	经常	jīngcháng	[1A 118]
Friday	星期五	xīngqīwǔ	[1A 158]
friend	朋友	péngyou	[1A 41]
fruit	水果	shuǐguǒ	7

English	Chinese	Pinyin	Page
fun	好玩儿	hǎowánr	32
G			
game, match, competition	比赛	bǐsài	[1A 118]
to get sick	生病	shēng bìng	125
to get up, to get out of bed	起床	qǐ chuáng	91
gift	礼物	lǐwù	[1A 168]
to give (a gift)	送	sòng	[1A 191]
to give; for, to	给	gěi	[1A 205]
to go	去	qù	[1A 114]
to go running; running	跑步	pǎo bù	47
to go to a class, to begin a class, to be in class	上课	shàng kè	74
good-looking, nice-looking (used for people and things)	好看	hǎokàn	[1A 191]
goodbye, see you again	再见	zàijiàn	[1A 21]
grades, score, achievement	成绩	chéngjì	199
grammar	语法	yǔfǎ	165
the Great Wall	长城	Chángchéng	27
guitar	吉他	jítā	[1A 133]
guzheng	古筝	gǔzhēng	[1A 133]
H			
half, half an hour	半	bàn	91
happy	快乐	kuàilè	[1A 216]
happy, pleased	高兴	gāoxìng	77
to have	有	yǒu	[1A 37]

English	Chinese	Pinyin	Page
to have a fever	发烧	fā shāo	125
to have a vacation (or holiday), to have time off	放假	fàng jià	199
to have free time, to be free	有空	yǒu kòng	[1A 158]
to have fun, to play, to hang out	玩儿	wánr	195
he, him	他	tā	[1A 37]
head	头	tóu	125
hello	你好	nǐ hǎo	[1A 21]
hello (over the phone)	喂	wéi	[1A 182]
to help	帮	bāng	151
here, over here	这儿	zhèr	[1A 114]
history	历史	lìshǐ	73
to hit, to play (basketball, ping-pong)	打	dǎ	[1A 109]
home	家	jiā	[1A 94]
homework	作业	zuòyè	91
to hope, to wish; hope	希望	xīwàng	199
hot	热	rè	120
hot pot	火锅	huǒguō	12
How is...?; How about it? Is it OK? How does that sound?	怎么样	zěnmeyàng	77
how many	几	jǐ	[1A 57]
hungry	饿	è	120

I

English	Chinese	Pinyin	Page
I, me	我	wǒ	[1A 21]

English	Chinese	Pinyin	Page
idea	主意	zhǔyi	[1A 168]
if	如果	rúguǒ	151
important	重要	zhòngyào	74
in that case, then, so	那	nà	[1A 168]
indoor court or field (for playing sports)	馆	guǎn	[1A 118]
interesting, fun	有意思	yǒuyìsi	[1A 114]
Isabella Lopez (a person's name)	林春月	Lín Chūnyuè	[1A 37]
it (used for animals and things)	它	tā	[1A 67]
J			
to join	加入	jiārù	189
June	六月	liùyuè	[1A 163]
K			
to kick, to play (soccer)	踢	tī	[1A 109]
to know	知道	zhīdào	[1A 89]
to know (a person), to recognize	认识	rènshi	189
L			
late	晚	wǎn	115
to learn, to study	学	xué	[1A 84]
Li (surname, sometimes spelled Lee)	李	Lǐ	[1A 141]
to like	喜欢	xǐhuan	[1A 62]
to listen to, to hear	听	tīng	[1A 141]
literature	文学	wénxué	73
to look at, to watch, to read, to see	看	kàn	[1A 62]

English	Chinese	Pinyin	Page
M			
to make a dish (of food)	做菜	zuòcài	[1A 205]
to make a phone call	打电话	dǎ diànhuà	[1A 205]
many, much, lots	多	duō	[1A 216]
Martin Lopez (a person's name)	林马丁	Lín Mǎdīng	[1A 37]
math	数学	shùxué	69
meal, cooked rice	饭	fàn	12
(measure word for a course)	门	mén	69
(measure word for books)	本	běn	[1A 186]
(measure word for clothing)	件	jiàn	[1A 191]
(measure word for kinds, sorts, types)	种	zhǒng	[1A 205]
(measure word for people and many everyday objects)	个	gè	[1A 57]
(measure word for plates of food)	份	fèn	[1A 212]
(measure word for some animals)	只	zhī	[1A 67]
meat (frequently pork)	肉	ròu	[1A 212]
to meet (up), to meet with	见面	jiàn miàn	195
to meet with, to see	见	jiàn	[1A 182]
minute	分	fēn	91
to mistakenly think, to assume incorrectly	以为	yǐwéi	165
month, moon	月	yuè	[1A 163]
mood, state of mind	心情	xīnqíng	77
more and more	越来越	yuè lái yuè	175
morning (before noon)	上午	shàngwǔ	[1A 182]

English	Chinese	Pinyin	Page
most, -est	最	zuì	69
mother, mom	妈妈	māma	[1A 57]
movie, motion picture	电影	diànyǐng	[1A 158]
music	音乐	yīnyuè	[1A 141]
musical instrument	乐器	yuèqì	[1A 133]
must, have to, need to	得	děi	96
N			
name	名字	míngzi	[1A 31]
(a name)	小明	Xiǎomíng	[1A 67]
neighborhood, apartment complex	小区	xiǎoqū	[1A 94]
nervous, anxious	紧张	jǐnzhāng	77
new	新	xīn	189
new words, vocabulary	生词	shēngcí	175
next	下个	xià ge	[1A 163]
night, evening	晚上	wǎnshàng	[1A 182]
nine	九	jiǔ	[1A 19]
no, not	不	bù	[1A 21]
noodles	面条	miàntiáo	[1A 212]
noon	中午	zhōngwǔ	[1A 182]
to not have	没有	méiyǒu	[1A 37]
not really, not very	不太	bú tài	[1A 62]
not until, only then	才	cái	91
now, at this time	现在	xiànzài	[1A 94]

English	Chinese	Pinyin	Page
O			
o'clock (literally, dot or point)	点	diǎn	91
older brother	哥哥	gēge	[1A 57]
older sister	姐姐	jiějie	[1A 57]
the Olympic Games	奥运会	Àoyùnhuì	52
one	一	yī	[1A 18]
or (in questions)	还是	háishi	[1A 89]
to order (food)	点	diǎn	[1A 205]
outdoor court or field (for sports)	场	chǎng	[1A 114]
P			
to pack (up), to tidy (up), to put things away	收拾	shōushi	151
person, people	人	rén	[1A 84]
pet (animal)	宠物	chǒngwù	[1A 67]
ping-pong, table tennis; ping-pong ball	乒乓球	pīngpāngqiú	[1A 109]
plan; to plan	计划	jìhuà	146
(a point in) time, moment	时候	shíhou	102
polite; to be polite/courteous	客气	kèqi	169
to practice; exercises	练习	liànxí	175
precisely, exactly	就	jiù	169
to preview, to study (materials not yet taught in class)	预习	yùxí	146
problem, question	问题	wèntí	141
pronunciation; to pronounce	发音	fāyīn	175
to pull, to play	拉	lā	[1A 133]

English	Chinese	Pinyin	Page
Q			
question, problem (in homework or on a test)	题	tí	169
(question word)	吗	ma	[1A 21]
quite, fairly, pretty, rather	挺	tǐng	77
R			
recently	最近	zuìjìn	189
to rest, to take a break	休息	xiūxi	120
restaurant	饭馆	fànguǎn	[1A 212]
to return, to go back	回	huí	199
to review, to study (materials already taught)	复习	fùxí	14
right, correct	对	duì	[1A 84]
roast duck	烤鸭	kǎoyā	12
S			
same, alike; as...as	一样	yíyàng	102
to say, to speak	说	shuō	73
school	学校	xuéxiào	[1A 94]
school term, semester	学期	xuéqī	199
science	科学	kēxué	69
to sell	卖	mài	[1A 137]
seven	七	qī	[1A 19]
she, her	她	tā	[1A 37]
should, ought to	应该	yīnggāi	194

English	Chinese	Pinyin	Page
simple	简单	jiǎndān	[1A 186]
to sing (a song)	唱歌	chàng gē	194
six	六	liù	[1A 19]
to sleep	睡觉	shuì jiào	91
so, therefore	所以	suǒyǐ	[1A 216]
soccer; soccer ball	足球	zúqiú	[1A 109]
some	有的	yǒude	102
some, a few	些	xiē	175
sports, exercise	运动	yùndòng	[1A 118]
to start, to begin; beginning	开始	kāishǐ	91
still, yet	还	hái	141
store, shop	店	diàn	[1A 137]
to strum, to pluck, to play	弹	tán	[1A 133]
student	学生	xúeshēng	[1A 21]
studies; to study, to learn	学习	xuéxí	146
to swim; swimming	游泳	yóu yǒng	47
T			
tasy, delicious	好吃	hǎochī	[1A 205]
to teach	教	jiāo	[1A 141]
teacher	老师	lǎoshī	[1A 21]
television	电视	diànshì	[1A 62]
to tell	告诉	gàosu	146
Temple of Heaven	天坛	Tiāntán	27

English	Chinese	Pinyin	Page
ten	十	shí	[1A 19]
tennis; tennis ball	网球	wǎngqiú	[1A 109]
thank you, thanks	谢谢	xièxie	[1A 141]
that	那	nà	[1A 89]
there is, there are	有	yǒu	[1A 114]
there, over there	那儿	nàr	[1A 114]
they, them (if anyone in the group is male)	他们	tāmen	[1A 41]
they, them (if everyone in the group is female)	她们	tāmen	[1A 41]
thing, matter, something to do	事	shì	[1A 182]
thing(s)	东西	dōngxi	151
thirsty	渴	kě	120
this	这	zhè	[1A 89]
three	三	sān	[1A 18]
time	时间	shíjiān	96
tired, tiring	累	lèi	96
today	今天	jīntiān	[1A 158]
together	一起	yìqǐ	102
tomorrow	明天	míngtiān	[1A 158]
too, extremely, overly	太	tài	32
tourist attraction/site, scenic spot	景点	jǐngdiǎn	27
twenty-one	二十一	èrshíyī	[1A 163]
two	二	èr	[1A 18]
two (used when counting things)	两	liǎng	[1A 59]

English	Chinese	Pinyin	Page
U			
to understand	懂	dǒng	165
United States of America	美国	Měiguó	[1A 84]
V			
very, really	很	hěn	[1A 62]
W			
to want (to do something)	想	xiǎng	[1A 114]
water	水	shuǐ	115
the Water Cube	水立方	Shuǐlìfāng	47
we, us	我们	wǒmen	[1A 41]
week	星期	xīngqī	[1A 94]
weekend	周末	zhōumò	[1A 163]
what	什么	shénme	[1A 31]
where	哪儿	nǎr	[1A 94]
which	哪	nǎ	69
who	谁	shéi	[1A 37]
why	为什么	wèishénme	[1A 216]
will	会	huì	151
to wish (well)	祝	zhù	[1A 216]
with, and; to	跟	gēn	102
(word added at the end of a sentence to add emphasis or excitement)	啊	a	[1A 137]
(word added at the end of a sentence to ask a follow-up question or to ask a question back to someone)	呢	ne	[1A 137]

English	Chinese	Pinyin	Page
(word added at the end of a sentence to make a suggestion or to soften the tone)	吧	ba	[1A 137]
(word that follows a verb and is used to introduce an impression)	起来	qǐ lái	165
(word that indicates an action is complete)	了	le	[1A 212]
(word used after a verb to indicate a past experience)	过	guò	169
(word used to link a verb to a description of the manner in which it was done)	得	de	189
to write	写	xiě	175
wrong, incorrect	错	cuò	169
Y			
yesterday	昨天	zuótiān	[1A 212]
you	你	nǐ	[1A 21]
you (plural)	你们	nǐmen	[1A 41]
younger brother	弟弟	dìdi	[1A 57]
younger sister	妹妹	mèimei	[1A 57]